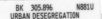

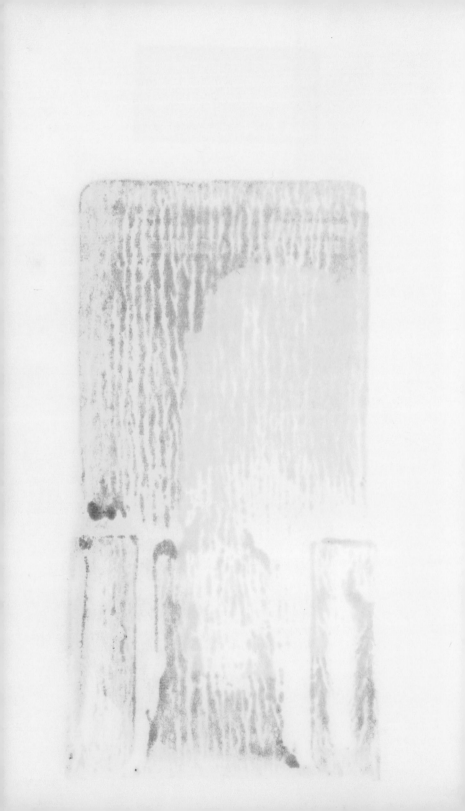

URBAN DESEGREGATION
NEGRO PIONEERS and Their WHITE NEIGHBORS

URBAN

DESEGREGATION

NEGRO PIONEERS

and Their

WHITE NEIGHBORS

L. K. NORTHWOOD

and ERNEST A. T. BARTH

UNIVERSITY OF WASHINGTON PRESS
SEATTLE · 1965

This research was substantially enabled by grants to the
authors from the Anti-Defamation League of B'nai B'rith,
The Division Fund, and the Field Foundation, Incorporated.

Acknowledgments

The title page of this book carries only the names of its two authors, thus credit for the assistance and cooperation obtained during every phase of the project must be given in this section. In truth, we have been assisted by more than 150 collaborators, and we would like to extend our thanks to all of them. The most important of these were the Negro families and their white neighbors whose accounts of their experiences provide the basis for this study. We hope that this book will partially repay them for their time and cooperation by helping to dispel some of the current myths about residential desegregation and thus contribute to the peaceful transformation of America from a segregated to a racially integrated society.

We are indebted to many organizations and their leaders for the social history of intergroup relations in Seattle. Valuable information was obtained from the files of the Seattle Civic Unity Committee and the Seattle Urban League through the cooperation of the respective executives, Miss Louise Blackham and Edwin Pratt. Glenn Mansfield of the Washington State Board Against Discrimination assisted with a review of the records of housing complaints filed with that body. Sidney Gerber, executive secretary of the Fair Housing Listing Service, provided full details about the housing transactions and policies of that organization, and later reviewed the manuscript for completeness and accuracy. Back issues of the monthly newsletters of the Seattle chapter of the National Association for the Advancement of Colored People and the Christian Friends for Racial Equality provided many valuable details. Interviews were conducted with Randolph Carter and Mrs. Walter G. Hiltner, then officers of those groups. On several occasions Edward Singler and Walter Hundley, officers in the Seattle Committee On Racial Equality, described the current activities of their organization. Study materials were also made available by Allen Potter of the planning division, United Good Neighbors of Seattle and King County.

Two Seattle organizations deserve special credit for the part they played in this project. The Greater Seattle Housing Council developed the design for this study in a pilot project under the direction of Ernest Barth. Officers of the Anti-Defamation League of B'nai B'rith, both regional and national, have furthered the research in many ways. A financial grant to aid in the analysis of the data was raised under the direction of Seymour Kaplan, Northwest regional director, and Howard Pruzan, then chairman of the board. National staff members Oscar Cohen and Morton Sobell reviewed the original outline of the book and its revisions. All four have contributed suggestions to improve the quality of the report and to secure for it a wide audience.

Additional assistance in the form of grants was obtained from The Field Foundation, Inc., and The Division Fund. In particular, Robert Klein of the latter organization provided much support and encouragement to the authors at critical phases of the study.

The research was advanced through the careful work of several University of Washington students. Interviewing assistance was provided by Reuel Amdur, Gilbert Arthur, Robert Barker, Frances Rideout Coughlin, Charlotte Donaldson, George Ferguson, Matthew Grieve, Harold Huebner, Clifford Hussey, Edmund Machamer, and Robert White, all of the School of Social Work. Interviews were also conducted by members of a sociology class studying the Negro community. The first comprehensive analysis of interviews with the Negro families and their neighbors was carried out by Reuel Amdur and was reported in his thesis. Subsequently he has been most generous in giving time to advise and to criticize this manuscript. Mrs. Coughlin, Mrs. Donaldson, and Mr. Ferguson spent many hours in a systematic analysis of the minutes of intergroup agencies and in a study of other historical documents of the intergroup agencies.

Louise Klein, Judith Gerhold, and Robert Reed served as research assistants and critics. We also wish to thank our wives, Olga Northwood and Grace Barth, for their careful and critical reading of the several drafts of this manuscript.

Technical advice in the conduct of the study was received from several members of the University of Washington sociology department. Walter B. Watson and Vincent Miller assisted with the population statistics. The map was prepared by the Office of Population Research under the direction of Calvin Schmid. The first typing of the manuscript was done under the careful supervision of Edith Carlson of the School of Social Work. We would like to extend particular thanks to Otto Larsen, director of the Institute for Sociological Research, and Ruth Berndahl for their assistance in the preparation of the final draft of the manuscript.

Contents

	Introduction: An Overview of the Problem	xi
ONE	Seattle	3
TWO	Case Studies of Six Neighborhoods	9
THREE	Who Are the Pioneers?	25
FOUR	The Housing Transaction	30
FIVE	The Neighborhood Response to Its First Pioneer Family	36
SIX	The Neighborhood Integration Process	47
SEVEN	The Activities of the Antidiscrimination Network	56
EIGHT	Conclusions: Program for Action Now	64
	Appendix A	89
	Appendix B	105
	Notes	109
	Bibliography	121

Introduction: An Overview of the Problem

THE STRATEGY of housing desegregation has received increased attention in recent years, first, as an end in itself, and second, because the formation and consolidation of ghetto conditions in the large central cities of the nation is threatening to negate programs for the desegregation of schools and other community facilities.

Logically, there are two strategies for housing desegregation, both of which are invested with many difficulties. Either Negroes can move away from geographical areas of high Negro density, or whites can move into them. This study will report on the first of these strategies, sometimes called "pioneering."

It tells the story of fifteen neighborhoods which received their first Negro family during the past five years.* The story is drawn from interviews with the Negro pioneers in each situation and five white families living nearby.[1] The history of the process is narrated in case studies, which are placed in the context of Seattle race relations, population movement, and social agency services. We are pointing toward answering such questions as: What are the potentials of the pioneering strategy for housing desegregation? What can be asked of the Negro family, and what should be asked of the social agencies and citizen groups concerned about chauvinism and the growth of residential segregation?

---

* In this report, the term neighborhood refers to a geographical area in which our informants lived, usually stretching for no more than three or four blocks, and within easy walking distance of all parts. Usually this term means that there are common interests and shared associations among the persons residing in the area. The neighborhoods in our sample vary in social integration, as will be indicated in the report.

There are several connotations to the term pioneering. One of these is that the new minority resident is making a *dangerous* foray into strange territory; our study suggests that this seldom is so in Seattle. Another is that the newcomer is the *first* of his kind in the territory. This is true of our study; however, in many cities the Negro pioneer may be returning to residential areas in which Negroes lived fifty or seventy-five years ago—before the lines of residential segregation were so firmly drawn. A third connotation is that the pioneer is an *advance agent.*

Is pioneering the first step in the desegregation process? This question will be answered only by history. The members of our sample do not elect to assume this stance, although pioneering itself has considerable symbolic significance for desegregation. It demonstrates that Negroes can successfully live and be accepted in white residential areas. This provides tangible evidence for others who need encouragement to make a similar move. It can disabuse many current half-truths and myths about Negro neighbors.

In examining the strategy of pioneering, we can also provide a preview of general problems of desegregation and the methods of meeting them. Such knowledge is essential to urban renewal in a democracy. During the past decade, urban renewal clearance projects have dispossessed hundreds of thousands of families living in the slum core of the city, over half of these being Negroes. For example, in New York City, almost eighty thousand persons were moved during the five-year period between 1954 and 1959. In Philadelphia, sixty-six thousand families have been displaced since 1949, more from highway construction and code enforcement programs than from federally aided clearance projects. In Providence, Rhode Island, 90 per cent of the Negro population will be transplanted by projects already approved. These are not extreme examples, but a part of a pattern that applies to most of the nation's large cities.

If these hundreds of thousands of minority families are not to be shifted from place to place in racial ghettos, it will be necessary to work out methods for the orderly desegregation of residential areas which are now all-white. Many findings from this study of fifteen neighborhoods can be applied to the general problem.

Our fifteen cases are placed in a framework of the neighborhood integration process. We ask the general questions: Is the neighborhood a viable interacting social entity? How is the newcomer initiated and absorbed into the area where his home is located? Sociological research about migration and urban life customarily has been weighted toward the examination of broad-scale patterns of land use and population movement, on the one hand, or with specialized institutional developments, on the other. There are few empirical studies of the detailed process of how change and social integration takes place at the neighborhood level. This is a modest step in that direction.

METHODS OF STUDY

The study of first Negro residents and their white neighbors presents many research problems.[2] First, the Negro newcomers must be located. Where there is a great outcry over their arrival, they can be easily identified. Our study shows that even where there was neighborhood protest, it was hardly visible in the larger community. In some cases, the Negro family blended into the existing neighborhood with as few difficulties as did whites.

For these reasons, the discovery of Negro newcomers is not always easy. We obtained our sample by searching the records of human relations agencies, from personal knowledge, from Negro informants, and from schools when a new Negro child first attended class. All of the twenty-six families located in this way were asked for an interview; two declined.

Second, the Negro family must consent before any of their white neighbors could be interviewed. The study was conducted under academic auspices by persons who could be vouched for by human relations agencies, and only one interracial couple, very new to their neighborhood, asked the research team not to interview their white neighbors. The final sample, based on fifteen neighborhoods, includes the Negro family, three white neighbors next-door or across the street, one white neighbor a block away, and another three blocks away. Thus, there are six interviews for each of fifteen neighborhoods. In addition, the team interviewed nine other Negro families where no attempt was made to secure white respondents as well.

The research team always informed Negro families about the purpose of the study, i.e., to record their experiences in neighborhood desegregation and to assess what helped and what hindered the process. On the other hand, the interviewer initially made a special effort to disguise the main purpose of the study from white respondents until he had secured information from them concerning their own experiences in moving into the neighborhood, their assessment of its friendliness, their own and their family's involvement in neighborhood organizations, and some other relevant items. Then he queried them about the neighborhood in an open-ended question:

> Suppose for awhile that a good friend of yours has been offered an opportunity to move into this neighborhood. Let's say he doesn't know anything about the neighborhood or about the people who live here. He's interested in finding out something about the different kinds of people who live here, how they get along together, and how he'll like them. So he asks you: "What are the people in this neighborhood like?"

If extensive probing failed to identify the presence of Negroes in the neighborhood, the interviewer asked: "Are there any Negro families living in this neighborhood?" A negative answer to this question would signal the interviewer to terminate after asking for a few personal data statistics. If the neighbor gave an affirmative answer, the interviewer would then ask a long sequence of questions about the move-in of the Negro and the neighborhood response.[3]

Both Negroes and whites were asked many parallel questions. From their answers, we derived a composite account of the desegregation process, which was supplemented on some occasions with newspaper clippings, social agency case records, and other documents.[4]

The research team visited each white family once, the Negro families twice, with the second visit coming about a year after the first. During the second visit, the interviewer queried the Negro family about prior interracial background, recent neighborhood developments, and about continuing associations with the "minority community."

The reliability of the questionnaire was enhanced by careful pretesting and by training of interviewers. The final interview schedule had also been pretested in an earlier form in a study carried out for the Greater Seattle Housing Council.[5]

There are definite limitations to this study, and the findings should be carefully tempered by these limitations. These are accounts of neighborhoods where the entry of the Negro family has been "successful"—successful in the sense that the family had secured a home, moved in, and stayed for a period of at least six months. Several sources, including the successful "pioneers," show good evidence that many minority families try to secure such housing and fail. Thus, this survey does not include unsuccessful pioneers. The accounts also are limited by the accuracy of the respondents' memories and by their willingness to talk. In most cases, both members of the minority family were present at the interview. One would frequently supplement the other's account. No one knows what was missed by the absence of a family member from the interview. Again, the sample of white respondents, especially those to be located one block and three blocks away from the residence of the Negro newcomer, was subject to interviewer choice, for the interviewer was allowed to pick a person to provide the information. In the case of the Reed family (see p. 21), the neighborhood was quite hostile and even a skilled interviewer experienced much difficulty in securing necessary white respondents. In general, however, interviews were completed with the first person asked, and no interview, once started, was terminated before all the information was secured.

A further limitation of this study is that it focuses attention on that segment of the Negro population which Frazier has labeled the "black bourgeoisie." [6] Most American Negroes presently do *not* fall in this category, although the past thirty years—marked by regional decentralization, rapid urbanization, and educational and occupational advancement—suggests that it will be an expanding and an increasingly important segment.[7] In addition, this segment of the Negro population will become more significant as attention is focused on developing adequate devices for assisting in their moving from urban renewal sites and other relocation areas.

URBAN DESEGREGATION
NEGRO PIONEERS and Their WHITE NEIGHBORS

GREATER SEATTLE AREA

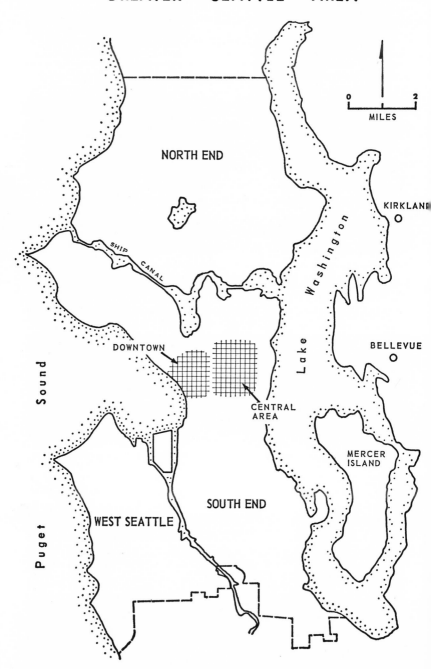

CHAPTER ONE

Seattle

THE SETTING for this study is Seattle, Washington. Geographically, Seattle is located in a far corner of the United States. It is about eleven hundred miles west of Denver, Colorado—the next largest city of its size to the east. It is nine hundred land miles north of San Francisco. Bounded on one side by the high reaches of the Cascade Range and on the other by the rain forests of the Olympic Peninsula and the Pacific Ocean, it is the stopping-off point for Alaska and the Arctic. Because of its somewhat isolated position, writers have often stated that Seattle has been able to avoid many of the conditions and problems that plague most large American cities.

It will become evident in the following analysis that Seattle's somewhat isolated position has *not* led to unique developments in minority housing or neighborhood integration. Seattle, like all major cities in the United States, has experienced a growth in the number and percentage of Negro residents. These residents tend to be concentrated in a limited area of the city—an area which contains a greater proportion of blighted houses than the city as a whole. The annual income of Negroes and other minorities is not sufficient to permit large numbers to purchase or rent adequate housing. Furthermore, prejudice and discrimination place all the city's minorities at a disadvantage in securing housing in many sections of the city.

IS THE MINORITY AREA BECOMING A NEGRO GHETTO?

By 1960, Negroes had become the largest colored minority in the city of Seattle. Numbering 26,901 persons, they comprised 4.83 per cent of the total population. Left behind in numbers and

3

proportions were the other colored races: American Indians, Japanese, Chinese, Filipinos, Koreans, Asian Indians, and Malayans. All together, the other colored races numbered 19,627 persons, 3.52 per cent of the city's inhabitants. Seattle's foreign-born white minorities, however, still exceeded the nonwhite minorities by a few thousands.[1]

The emergence of the Negro as Seattle's largest colored minority is part of the movement that has characterized all large cities in the United States. The rate of growth of the Negro population in most major centers has been nothing short of explosive. In Seattle, for example, the white population increased by about 3 per cent between 1950 and 1960. During the same period, Negro and other colored minorities increased by about 71 per cent. The growth in the city between 1950 and 1960 was 32,212, of which 12,851 were whites, 11,235 Negroes, and 8,126 other colored minorities.[2]

Seattle's nonwhite minorities are not distributed evenly throughout the city and neighboring King County. There are only 904 Negroes living in suburban King County as compared with 26,901 in the central city—about one Negro in the surrounding county for every thirty in the city. The other colored minorities are also concentrated in Seattle, with the ratio being five in the city to one in the rest of the county. Within the city limits, the colored races tend to be concentrated in a few localities near to the center.

Historically, Seattle's first Negro population lived downtown. In about 1890, William Gross, a wealthy Negro, acquired a large tract of land in the vicinity of East Madison and Twenty-third Avenue. Many Negro families followed Gross to "the hill" where they built their own homes and became the founders of what is called the Central Area in this book. A second Negro center developed later in the Jackson Street area; this area contained a more transient population, largely male, who worked on ships and trains, or as day laborers, waiters, or entertainers. Since that time the two centers have tended to merge and to expand in other directions, mainly to the south along the thoroughfares leading to the Boeing Company plant.

The United States Census has divided the city into 118 tracts. In 1960, there was not a single census tract that did not contain at least one nonwhite resident, and all but eighteen of the tracts included at least one Negro resident. [3] Despite this thin scattering of colored families in all sections of the city, the great bulk were located in a few tracts. About three quarters of all Negro residents lived in nine census tracts located in four square miles—east of the central business district of Seattle to the shore of Lake Washington, from East Roy and East Mercer on the north to South Dearborn and South Irving streets to the south. A similar concentration exists nearby for the Japanese, Chinese, and Filipino minorities. Statistics based on city blocks also indicate a heavy concentration of nonwhites in these areas.[4]

The concentration of nonwhites has not diminished since 1950; it has markedly increased. From 1950 to 1960, the proportion of Seattle's Negro population living in five of these census tracts increased from 44 per cent to 55 per cent. The proportion living in all nine tracts increased from 66 per cent to 75 per cent. In 1950 there were only nine 100-per-cent nonwhite blocks; by 1960, there were thirty-eight. In 1950 there were seventy-seven blocks with three quarters or more of the dwelling units nonwhite; by 1960 there were 298 such blocks and many more that contained almost as high a proportion of nonwhites and appeared to be well on the path toward becoming ghettos. Thus, while the nonwhite population of the city increased by a little less than three quarters (71 per cent) between 1950 and 1960, the number of totally or predominantly nonwhite blocks almost quadrupled. Although the Negro population increased rapidly, the number of Negroes residing in the fifty-four census tracts north of the Lake Washington Ship Canal (Seattle's white North End) actually decreased between 1950 and 1960.

The analysis so far reveals a Negro community in Seattle which is rapidly growing in size; it further demonstrates the emergence of a relatively well-defined minority area, which may become a full-fledged Negro ghetto if the city does not take adequate steps to stop this development.

RACE RELATIONS IN SEATTLE—A HISTORICAL OVERVIEW

In comparison with other large American cities, the current living conditions and climate of opinion about race relations in Seattle are usually considered good. In the long view of history, however, colored minorities in Seattle have not always fared so well. Traditions of prejudice and discrimination crop up in the present. Therefore, a brief review of some major events in the city's history provides a context for viewing this study of neighborhood desegregation.[5]

It is common knowledge that the Puget Sound region was taken at gunpoint from its first large colored minority, the Indians.[6] Not so widely known is the fact that the first Negro pioneers, who traveled by wagon train across the country into what was then the Oregon Territory, were forced to move on by an act of the Territorial Legislature which made their settlement illegal.[7] Some of these Negroes went on to Vancouver, British Columbia, and later became Seattle's "First Citizens."

During Seattle's early decades, the largest colored minority was Chinese. Brought into the Northwest by the thousands to help build the railroads, they flocked, fifteen thousand strong, into hop fields, mines, fish canneries, and sawmills when the job was done. The Chinese also went to the cities, such as Seattle, to do whatever work they could find for any wage that would keep them alive.[8] This cheap labor definitely threatened the living standards of white workers, and they decided to force the Chinese out. When the federal government and the railroads refused to remove the Chinese, in February, 1866, the workers did the job. The Chinese of Seattle were rounded up and marched to the *Queen of the Pacific* about to depart for San Francisco. Within a few weeks, there was hardly a Chinese in the area.

There is a more recent parallel. In 1940, the Japanese, numbering 6,975, were the largest colored minority residing in Seattle. After Pearl Harbor, prejudice against the Japanese mounted until 1942, when 110,000 persons on the West Coast were placed in internment camps and relocated.[9] Seattle's Japanese citizens were forcibly evacuated from their homes within a few days in accordance with the following rationale: [10]

> In the war in which we are now engaged racial affinities are not severed by migration. The Japanese race is an enemy race and while many second and third generation Japanese born on United States soil, possessed of United States citizenship, have become "Americanized," the racial strains are undiluted. . . . That Japan is allied with Germany and Italy in this struggle is no ground for assuming

that any Japanese, barred from assimilation by convention as he is, though born and raised in the United States, will not turn against this nation when the test of loyalty comes. It, therefore, follows that along the vital Pacific Coast over 112,000 potential enemies of Japanese extraction, are at large today. There are indications that these are organized and ready for concerted action at a favorable opportunity. The very fact that no sabotage has taken place to date is a disturbing and confirming indication that such action will be taken.

Aside from suffering the stigma of being branded as traitors without a shred of evidence, it is estimated that the Japanese-Americans averaged losses of nearly $10,000 per family from property sold in desperation at a fraction of its worth, property deterioration, loss of wages, and the like.[11]

Antialien land laws, directed primarily at Orientals, have continued in effect in the state of Washington since their passage in the first quarter of the century.[12] These prohibit the lease or ownership of land by foreign-born Chinese, Japanese, and others. The latest attempt to remove this legislation by ballot failed in the 1962 elections, when the majority voted to uphold the discriminatory law.

Legislation against racial discrimination in housing has had almost as little success as the attempt to remove the antialien land laws. Sections of the state of Washington's antidiscrimination statute covering housing, passed some years earlier, were declared unconstitutional by the Washington State Supreme Court in 1961.[13] Subsequent efforts to pass an amended law in the state legislature failed. In 1964, a city ordinance prohibiting discrimination in housing was rejected by a substantial majority of voters in Seattle and nearby Tacoma. The failure of the Seattle ordinance was mitigated in part when the commissioners of King County enacted the first county fair-housing law in the United States, barring discrimination in the county's unincorporated areas.[14] At about the same time, Seattle became the last of the nation's cities of over five hundred thousand—excluding the Deep South—to establish a tax-supported human rights commission.

Such is the negative side of the history of race relations in Seattle. Yet despite these gross breaches of democracy, the minority populations, Oriental and Negro, have increased in numbers. The experiences to follow as reported from Seattle's pioneer neighborhoods show that housing desegregation is indeed moving ahead; and other developments are taking place in the metropolitan area that place it in the forefront of the nation—almost without the benefit of ameliorative legislation.

CHAPTER TWO

Case Studies of Six Neighborhoods

SEATTLE IS CALLED the "City of the Seven Hills." Thus, the hills and lakes split the city into the many different settings in which its residential neighborhoods are located. Built at different times, layer by layer, the typical appearance of the housing reflects the tastes of the original owners as mediated by the architect, the realtor, the city planner of the period. Most of all, the residential neighborhood is the embodiment of the people who live in it and of those who serve its churches, schools, shops, and clubs.

The following pages contain case vignettes of six of the fifteen neighborhoods studied. In each case, the initial desegregation will be described; this consists of an account of the entry of the Negro family and of the consequent neighborhood reactions. These six families have lived in their respective neighborhoods for periods ranging from five months to four years. We will make an assessment of each of the families to see how they have (or have not) become established in the fabric of neighborhood life.

Most of our fifteen cases are "success stories" both in terms of the initial desegregation and also in terms of the compatible neighborhood accommodation *for this family.* Therefore, three of the vignettes will describe reasonably easy entrance and neighborhood acceptance. The others tell of difficulties, either at the time of entry or later.

The three cases of easy entry point to different channels for desegregation. The Price family lives in a university district, and Mr. Price is a student of limited means, living in a temporary rented residence. The Prices benefit by the tolerance frequently found in university communities. The John family was able to find its home through the help of residents in the upper-middle-income neighborhood into which they moved; they were rapidly accepted and became integrated into the life of the neighborhood. The Parsons, both professional social workers, enjoyed the full help of the social agency communications system in finding their home and in becoming accepted there.

The Strong family had little difficulty in purchasing a home; but the animosities that were roused when they moved in still remained eighteen months later when they were interviewed. On the other hand, the Reeds had great difficulty securing a house in the upper-middle-income area where they wished to purchase. The vigorous opposition they encountered led to social-agency intervention. Three years later, however, the Reeds had become a part of the neighborhood network. The story of the Jones family, the final vignette, is one of continuing minor conflict from move-in to the final interview, four years later. It tells a story of difficult entry and limited acceptance for the Negro family.

Our procedure will be to present the bare details about each of the six cases. The following chapters summarize the findings of the study. A detailed account of the procedures for the selection and analysis of the six cases is included in the Appendix (pp. 105-7).

CASE 1: NEIGHBOR ACCOMMODATION IN A UNIVERSITY DISTRICT

Mr. and Mrs. Price, age thirty, have always lived in the Northwest. They have two sons, ten and eight. Mrs. Price works evenings to support the family while her husband is completing his college education. Their annual family income is about $3,500.

Selecting the home and neighborhood

The Prices selected this home mainly because it was near the University. The move came in 1960 after the Prices had lived in the nearby student housing project for some time. One day they saw a "for rent" sign in front of the house. Upon inquiry, they met the landlord, who rented the house to them immediately. The Prices have been pleased with everything: their landlord has always been cooperative in providing needed repairs; the children's schooling has been uninterrupted. Mr. Price feels that if Negroes have a positive, friendly attitude when moving into a white neighborhood, they will encourage a similar response. No social agencies were involved in the home-finding process.

Moving in

No opposition to the move-in was reported. One neighbor visited the Prices soon after their entry to welcome them, but the visit was not repeated. For some time Mr. Price and a neighbor exchanged visits until the neighbor moved away. In general, Mr. Price is preoccupied with his studies and his family; Mrs. Price works every evening. They received an invitation to join the PTA via a note which their children brought home from school. They attended once or twice. Mrs. Price was also asked to join a student-wives' organization, but this was difficult because of her work. The whole family attends a church in the University District to which they belonged before moving into this area. The Prices' association memberships are much the same as other students living in the neighborhood. Only one neighbor, who owned his own home, belonged to a local organization. Of the five white families, only one noted much visiting, and that usually occurred within the housing project among wives and students having the same academic interests. There is very little visiting between residents of the housing project and those living in the neighborhood outside the project.

Getting established

The Prices report that their children have experienced no hostility in the neighborhood or at school; they play daily with the children and get along well with the adult neighbors in the area. In return, however, only one neighbor reported that his children played with the Price children, and that was at school. Most of the children living nearby are quite young. The Prices' youngest child is a Cub Scout, and the father has gone along with his son to scouting activities, where both were well received. The older son has been unable to find an organized play group with boys of his own age.

Although presently the Prices do not exchange visits, they feel that the neighborhood is friendly. People smile and greet each other in passing. Shopkeepers are cordial. All of the neighbors expressed neutral attitudes toward the Price family. This reaction seemed to be qualified by the fact that all but one are renters, and the neighborhood is seen as temporary lodging. No one was concerned about having Negro neighbors. One said they should be treated "like any other family." Another said, "They should be left alone and not have any trouble caused them." Another view was that "persons should be pleasant to them and let them know that they are welcome." No one believed that the presence of the Price family had affected property values. Some neighbors felt, however, that the situation might be different in a different neighborhood, and the one owner in this sample expressed more concern than others.

It is evident that the Price family has been accepted by other residents of the area, although there is not much interaction. This is an example of interracial accommodation, which will be discussed later in the book.

CASE 2: A NEIGHBORHOOD IS PREPARED FOR INTEGRATION

At the time of the study Mr. and Mrs. John, ages thirty-four and thirty, and their four children, aged two weeks to four and one-half years, had lived in their neighborhood for over four years. Before moving into this neighborhood the family had lived in the central ghetto area of Seattle. Mr. John, a lawyer, was born in Georgia but spent most of his life in Delaware where his neighborhood and school contacts were mainly with Negroes. Mrs. John was born and reared in Hawaii. She graduated from the University of Hawaii, having majored in education, and in 1954 moved to Seattle. The family's average annual income is between $10,000 and $14,000.

Selecting the home and neighborhood

Several factors helped the Johns decide to move into this particular neighborhood. The house was located in a relatively wooded area which was covered with dense vegetation. It was also conveniently close to schools and shopping areas. Aside from liking the location, the couple felt that the house was a good buy and they also liked the owners. In fact, the owners had taken the house off the market while the John family were deciding whether they were going to buy it.

The family learned about the house through a "white" multiple-listing service and anticipated difficulty in getting their mortgage approved. However, because of the efforts of a friend, they experienced no difficulty. The people in the neighborhood agreed that from the time the Johns bought the home to the present, they have kept up the general maintenance of the grounds and have done some painting.

Moving in

There was no opposition to their moving into the neighborhood either on the part of individual neighbors or organized groups, although one elderly neighbor constructed a "spite" fence. Neither of the two distant neighbors interviewed knew, at the time of the study, that there were Negroes living in the vicinity. The three immediate neighbors, two of whom were buying their homes, had moved there after the John family. At the time they moved in, these people were concerned because there were Negroes living in the area. However, after talking with other Caucasian residents, they discovered that the John family was considered "one of the finest families in the neighborhood." This allayed their fears.

Getting established

People in the neighborhood consider it to be a friendly one where the people are interested in each other and willing to help one another. They were friendly, but not overly so. Neighborhood visiting occurred frequently among the wives and less among the husbands. Two of Mrs. John's immediate neighbors report exchanging visits with her frequently and the third visited occasionally. The husbands "drop in" once a month or less.

The incident which sparked the neighborhood visits occurred when one of the John children suffered a serious injury. One neighbor rushed the child and Mrs. John immediately to the hospital, while another stayed with the other children and finished up the housework. The Caucasian neighbors feel "friendly" or "very friendly" toward their Negro neighbors. On the other hand, the neighborhood considers this family to be an exception, and they are not viewed as "regular Negroes." One neighbor said that he did not want "lower class Negroes" in the neighborhood. Two of the families described Mrs. John as being light-skinned, and Hawaiian or Puerto Rican. All of the neighbors saw the John family as being "much the same as themselves." One stated that the Johns were actually above the rest of them. Two of the neighbors' children play regularly with the John children; the child of the third neighbor is too young to play with anyone. The John children fit into the neighborhood and often share meals in the homes of their playmates.

This pioneer family belongs to no local organizations, although they feel that they would be accepted if they would choose to join. As a matter of fact, none of the families interviewed in that neighborhood belonged to any organizations. Since the local Baptist church was convenient, the family joined, shifting their membership from one in the Central Area. Mr. John belonged to several metropolitan professional organizations, including the Kiwanis Club. He was an officer in the local Urban League, the Washington Children's Home Society, and the Medina Agency.

Neither in looking for their home nor in becoming established had the John family contacted any local human relations agency. However, they felt that when a minority family was moving into a previously all-Caucasian neighborhood, agencies should conduct a door-to-door educational program in order to discover and discuss neighborhood fears. None of the neighbors reported any contact with agency representatives before, during, or after their Negro neighbors moved in. There were mixed feelings about the merit of agency work in this area. Some had favorable attitudes, indicating that they felt such agency contacts could ease the transition. Others were neutral, and a few felt that agencies would do more harm than good.

All of the neighbors have a high opinion of the John family and the pioneers feel that they have made satisfactory adjustments in the neighborhood. They do not feel that property values in that area have decreased because of their presence nor did any of the neighbors seem concerned about this at the time of the study. If there was any change in neighborhood attitudes after their move, the pioneers felt that they had "become quite close" to several of their neighbors. After the first interviews were held, the John family moved to New York.

CASE 3: ASSISTANCE BY A HUMAN RELATIONS AGENCY

The Parsons family consists of Mr. and Mrs. Parsons, both age thirty. Mr. Parsons, a social agency executive, was born and reared in Florida. Mrs. Parsons grew up in Texas and is a group social worker. As children, both lived in integrated neighborhoods; however, they attended all-Negro schools. They both have advanced degrees. They were married and came to Seattle six years ago, lived in the center of the city for three and one half years, and then moved to their suburban home. The annual family income is between $10,000 and $14,000.

Selecting the neighborhood and home

The former owner had called a social agency and offered his home for sale on an open-market basis. This information came immediately to Mr. Parsons' attention. He had been looking for a home for his family, and after seeing the house, he bought it. The neighbors did not know that the new owners were Negroes until after they had moved in. Mr. Parsons believes that the neighborhood should not be given advance notice of such moves and that problems which might arise should be met after the Negro family moves in. No difficulty in financing occurred, and the purchase was completed by Caucasian friends without the aid of a real estate agent.

Moving in

The Parsons moved in on a Saturday. The next-door neighbors visited them over the back fence and came to their home to visit two days later. Several nights later another neighbor came to call and seemed favorably impressed by their social work background. The Parsons do not feel there was opposition to their arrival.

Soon after the entry, the minister of the local Episcopal church, which was in the process of forming, invited them to join the group. They joined, and both are now on church committees. Mrs. Parsons was asked to become a member of the District Scouting Committee. She attended several meetings, but because of time pressures found it necessary to resign.

Two of the three immediate neighbors had lived there at the

time the Parsons moved in; the third arrived two weeks later. One of the distant neighbors was unaware that a Negro family lived in the area. The older residents had been concerned. They were angry at the former owner because he did not inform them that he had sold to a Negro family. Later, however, they found the Parsons to be "nice people."

Getting established

There has been little visiting back and forth in this case. The next-door neighbor has taken packages for the Parsons, kept their mail, and watched their house when they went on vacation. Both Mr. and Mrs. Parsons work, and they have no children. They feel that these two factors have made it difficult to make friends in this neighborhood. They also feel that the general attitude of the neighbors has improved since they moved in. In Mr. Parsons' words, "They found out we don't have tails." A neighbor, whose property borders the Parsons, had never spoken with them until eighteen months later, when his dog wandered into their yard. This led to an initial conversation, and now they greet each other in passing. Another next-door neighbor has never spoken, but their daughter sold Bluebird mints to the Parsons.

All but one of the neighbors feel "neutral" about the Parsons, and all report no visiting with them. The Parsons are described as nice people who are quiet and keep to themselves. In general, there is not much visitation among neighbors, Negro or white in the area. However, several mentioned memberships in local churches and the PTA.

None of the neighbors felt that agencies should be involved in this kind of a situation because "this is a neighborhood problem and should be handled at that level."

The Parsons have adjusted well in the neighborhood, although there is not much interaction between them and their neighbors. They have a modern, well-furnished home and have put in a patio, put heat in the play room, and have connected with the sewer system. While they are meeting some passive hostility, the Parsons feel that as they are better known in the community this will disappear.

CASE 4: DIFFICULT ENTRY—NEIGHBORHOOD ACCOMMODATION

Mr. and Mrs. Strong, ages thirty-four and thirty-two, have two boys, ages fourteen and seven, and two girls, eleven and ten. They grew up in Washington, D.C., where many of their contacts were interracial. Mr. Strong completed the eleventh grade and is employed as a mechanic. His wife, a high school graduate, is a staff clerk for a public utilities firm. The annual family income is $9,000 to $10,000.

Selecting the home and neighborhood

A freeway construction program led the Strongs to move out of central Seattle. They saw this as an opportunity to secure less crowded quarters in the South End. The home they picked had been located previously by a Negro realtor, and they were able to make a down payment and move in with no difficulty whatsoever. But then the trouble started. Neighbors report that the house was sold to Negroes because the former owner wanted to spite the neighborhood. It was reported that the neighbors had successfully opposed in court the former owner's wishes to have the area rezoned for apartments.

Moving in

After the move, Mrs. Strong discovered she was living next to a fellow employee. Although they had been most friendly at work, this did not apply to neighboring. In fact, a new animosity was set up at work that did not end until her fellow employee quit. This opposition permeated the neighborhood. An offer was made by the local Community Club to buy the house from the Strongs. The two delegates from the Community Club who made the offer were Mrs. Strong's fellow worker and another next-door neighbor. Mrs. Strong suspected that the Community Club had been specially formed to buy them out, and interviews with the neighbors confirmed her assessment.

When the Strongs refused to sell, they were warned that they would be uncomfortable and that their children would be "miserable in the area." Hostile comments greeted them whenever they met these neighbors. One next-door neighbor, of Southern origin, built a tall fence to shut the Strongs out, and he painted it black on one side and white on the other. The fence stayed up for a short time—until the two hostile neighbors moved—and a new white occupant tore it down. During the whole period, different realtors called the Strongs daily to see if they would sell.

Not all the experiences of the Strongs were this unfriendly. The local Methodist minister visited them and offered membership in his church. Another nearby neighbor repeated this invitation. Now the Strongs' children have begun to attend, although their parents do not. The local PTA also asked Mrs. Strong to join, and she has attended several meetings.

Getting established

Neighborhood opposition has diminished since the most hostile families moved away. Some neighbors speak to the Strongs and some do not. This seems to be an individual matter. The Strongs feel that not much visiting occurs in this neighborhood, but their view is not shared by their immediate neighbors, who believe the opposite. The evidence is that there is more neighboring among the whites than there is between the races. However, Mrs. Strong works, thus reducing her time at home. Mr. Strong exchanged visits a few times with the man next door.

When the Strongs first moved in, neighborhood children were forbidden by their parents to play with the Negro children. Although this is no longer the case, play contacts seem to be infrequent except during the summer. Neighbors repeatedly commented on the "good manners" of the Strongs' children and also said that they were the only children in the neighborhood who do not cut across yards and who keep to themselves.

The immediate neighbors, with one exception, stated that they felt "friendly" about having the Strongs as neighbors at the time they were interviewed. The two distant neighbors did not positively know that there were Negroes living in the area, although more than three years had passed since their arrival. One of these distant neighbors mentioned that he suspected this was the case, since he had seen Negroes walking in the neighborhoods.

The Strongs have not joined as many local organizations as their neighbors. They were invited to join the PTA and have done so. Others living in the neighborhood about the same length of time belong to a greater number of local organizations.

The Strongs seem to have overcome the early resistance to their entry. This resistance apparently diminished when prejudiced neighbors moved away. In the process of becoming settled, the PTA and the Methodist church made friendly overtures, and the State Board Against Discrimination was alerted to trouble. Neither the Strongs nor their neighbors feel that social agencies could help much in the situation, and some thought that such help would do more harm than good. Although the initial resistance has dissipated and there is currently a residue of tolerance and friendliness for the Strongs among their immediate neighbors, the final product seems to be interracial accommodation rather than integration.

CASE 5: EASY ENTRY—CONTINUING CONFLICT IN THE LARGER NEIGHBORHOOD

The Reeds are both thirty-four, with twin sons, age six. Mr. Reed is a design engineer, earning about $12,000 yearly. After childhood in a small Negro community in Louisiana, he moved to the Midwest where he completed high school and college in integrated schools. His wife was also raised in the Midwest in a transitionary neighborhood in the process of changing from mainly white to Negro. Their first local residency was in the central Seattle ghetto area.

Selecting the home and neighborhood

The Reeds found their home only after an exhaustive search. They blocked off a map of the city, looked at ads, and consulted realtors. They wanted a home worth about $35,000 in which their investment would be reasonably secure for resale, if they should wish to move later on. Most realtors tried to discourage them in their hunt. Whenever they were turned down, they reported this to the State Board Against Discrimination, so that possible violators of the antidiscrimination law might be prosecuted.

The home they finally settled on was purchased through a Jewish real estate agent, who also helped arrange financing. They were able to assume the mortgage of the owner, who wished to build another house next-door to property purchased by the Reeds. This was a Jewish family, the Mortons, strongly opposed to discrimination in housing.

Moving in

In order to smooth the way for the new Negro family, the Mortons held a tea in their home and invited neighbors and the local pastor to meet the Reeds. This reception crystallized both support and opposition.

The opposition took the form of a petition campaign to prevent Mr. Morton from building his new home. It was also directed against the Reeds, whose home could be reached only by using a private road which crossed a neighbor's property. Permission to use the road had never been denied while the Mortons were living in the house. The opposition requested that the Seattle Planning Board deny the Mortons the right to build their new home and the Reeds the right to use the private road. At this time the Mortons asked Seattle Civic Unity and the American Civil Liberties Union for legal advice, and another neighbor called on the Seattle Urban League for help. This opposition campaign died out after the Planning Board rejected the neighbors' complaints. One neighbor asked the Real Estate Board for help; he was told that this was "blockbusting by the NAACP," but no further action was forthcoming.

Neither the Reeds, the Mortons, nor their neighbors were satisfied with the work of the human relations agencies. Some appreciated the intention to help, but felt that the agencies lacked the power to be effective. Some white neighbors believed the neighborhood should handle its problems without outside interference.

Getting established

When they first moved to the neighborhood, the Reeds were asked to join the PTA. They do not consider themselves "joiners" and have not taken up this invitation. On the whole, the neighborhood does not participate very much in local organizations.

Although there was opposition to the Reeds at first, it did not receive organized support from the outside. Nor has there been any hostility from the neighborhood shopkeepers. Both the Reeds' and the Mortons' children have from time to time been the objects of the neighborhood children's rock throwing and name calling. Mrs. Morton feels that her children have been ostracized at school because of their parents' stand. Two years after the event they were still being called "nigger lovers" and "reds." The Reeds do not feel that their children have more of a problem than might be expected in any large city.

There is still opposition in the larger community outside the cul-de-sac which contains the homes of the Reeds, Mortons, and four other neighbors, but there seems to be warm acceptance close at home. The Reed children do not play with their neighbors; however, there is a large age difference. A neighbor's daughter occasionally baby-sits for the Reeds.

Both the Reeds and their neighbors say that this is not the kind of neighborhood where frequent visiting occurs. This suits Mr. Reed well, because he is not very outgoing and sociable. However, the interviews indicate that informal visiting takes place once a week or more among the neighbors—apparently without distinction as to race.

Mrs. Reed and other mothers cooperate in driving their young children to school. The men borrow tools and share work on the alley, but there is little formal social life. Visits are initiated equally by the Negro family and their neighbors.

The next-door neighbors feel "friendly" or "very friendly" toward the Reeds. Two others see them as being like other neighbors. One says they are different in that they are above most people in the neighborhood both intellectually and emotionally.

Apparently the Reeds are well accepted by those nearby. They have made several home improvements, and no one seems to feel that property values have dropped because of their presence. The main opposition, if any, comes from the larger neighborhood rather than the immediate one.

CASE 6: THEY BUILT A NEW HOME
AND WEATHERED THE CONFLICT

Mr. and Mrs. Jones are thirty-six and thirty-one, with a seven-year-old son and a two-year-old daughter. Mr. Jones has a tenth grade education and works night shift in a government job. His wife, who has completed three years of college, works for a local apparel shop. The family income is approximately $9,500 a year.

Although the Joneses have been Seattle residents for several years, Mrs. Jones was born and reared in Florida and Mr. Jones in the Bahamas. Both report that most of their early associations were predominantly with Negroes.

Selecting the area

The Jones family solved their long search for a nice home in a quiet, uncongested area by purchasing a double-sized lot in the southern part of Seattle. Although their search had been long and realtors had told them frequently that homeowners would not sell to a Negro, they had no difficulties in purchasing the lot through a Negro realtor, nor did they have trouble in obtaining financing.

While his home was under construction, Mr. Jones received his first visit—a friendly one from a neighbor to welcome him. Apparently this is the usual neighborhood practice.

Moving in

During the first two months after moving in, it soon became evident that several neighbors were unhappy about the Jones's arrival. One neighbor accused Mr. Jones of picking fruit from his tree, although it turned out that the tree was on the Jones's property. Someone drove a car through the hedge. Another threw lawn trimmings on Jones's property. This was halted only when the trash was thrown back where it came from. Another neighbor, a city employee, made loud derogatory statements about his Negro neighbors. This ended only after Mr. Jones's lawyer was able to bring pressure to bear at City Hall. Apparently the neighbors also instructed their children not to play with the Negro children. At first, this took the form of calling across the street in friendly fashion, "Hi, Nigger," to little Jimmy Jones. Later this became more antagonistic roughhousing at the school playground.

The newcomers considered these events as "little things," but Mrs. Jones was quite incensed that her father-in-law, on a visit, would be subjected to insults that never would be tolerated at his home in the Bahamas. They believe most of the opposition came from the younger married set, jealous of the higher value of the Jones's new home, which they have continued to improve and which is above the neighborhood level in construction and spaciousness. The Joneses do not believe that the opposition to their entry was formally organized by any outside group, and this opinion is also held by their neighbors—although all were quite frank in stating that there was opposition in the beginning. It might be noted that the Jones family is the only one interviewed at any time during the study that reported hostility on the part of shopkeepers.

Getting established

Residents of the Jones's neighborhood are not "joiners" of local groups, and most families do not belong to local organizations. The Joneses were invited to the PTA and became members. Other than this, Mr. Jones has remained active in several organizations concerned with race relations—the NAACP, Urban League, and Aid for Africa. When they go to church, it is in the Central Area, and Mrs. Jones belongs to the Women's Circle of her church.

Although there is a dearth of formal organizational activities in the area, all families reported neighborly visits, but they do not cut across the color line. The white families in the sample say they do not exchange visits with the Negro family. This was verified partially by Mr. Jones, who said he was the one to do any visiting, but that there was not much of this because both he and Mrs. Jones work during the day. One new, young couple exchanged visits with them, and for this the wife was dropped by the local "coffee klatch."

A similar situation is reported among the children. Although Mrs. Jones said her child plays with other neighborhood children now, her neighbors disagree. This is partly because of a difference in ages; but one mother told how the neighbors became so angry with her because she let her child play with Jimmy Jones that she finally had to forbid it. This is one reason that she would like to move out of the neighborhood.

When the Joneses first moved into the neighborhood, many white families had talked of moving out. No one had done so at the time of the interview, four years later. However, some disgruntlement and resentment still simmered. Two immediate neighbors said they were strongly opposed to having Negroes living in their neighborhood and were still planning to move. Two others were neutral. Another family, living three blocks from the Joneses, did not know a Negro resided in the neighborhood although they had been there eight years, belonged to the local church, and reported active visiting with their neighbors.

After four years, the open hostility which greeted the Jones family on their arrival has subsided, but passive hostility remains. Mr. Jones was able to cope with neighbor aggression pretty much on his own, after he had requested aid from the NAACP and the Urban League, who, according to his account, "passed the buck." The Joneses are described by all their neighbors, including the hostile ones, as being neat and clean in personal appearance, careful in caring for their home, industrious, and willing to keep to themselves. Because of the quiet neighborhood and the convenient school for their son, the Joneses prefer their new home to their former apartment. They miss the convenience of central Seattle—so near to work, shopping centers, "socials," Mrs. Jones's church, and her beauty parlor. They feel their son is reasonably happy and accepted at school. They have not contemplated moving, but look forward to gradual changes in the neighborhood that will permit them to become more a part of it.

CHAPTER THREE

Who Are the Pioneers?

THE SHORT narratives of the last chapter sketched a brief picture of six neighborhoods which had received their first Negro resident during the past five years. In the chapters that follow, our account will be broadened to the fifteen neighborhoods about which we have information from both the Negro family and five white neighbors. Each chapter will deal with information that is relevant to understanding the neighborhood integration process. In some places, the basic survey of fifteen neighborhoods will be supplemented by additional interview data.

In this chapter we will comment on the kind of people who become pioneers in neighborhood desegregation. Interviews with nine other pioneers will be added to the basic sample of fifteen neighborhoods. Thus, in all, we have the experiences of twenty-four Negro families and seventy-five white neighbors. The data on neighborhoods can be supplemented by the 1960 United States Census, thus providing a more adequate statistical description of pioneer neighborhoods and ghetto neighborhoods, and of the entire city of Seattle.[1]

ECONOMIC POSITION

Into what kinds of neighborhoods do the pioneers move? Data show that they are somewhat more prosperous than those in the city as a whole. The median family income of these neighborhoods was $7,171 in 1960, but, on an average, the new Negro families earned $9,500 that year. Thus, it appears that they were more prosperous than most of their white neighbors. The pioneer families also earned about $4,000 more each year than other nonwhite families living in Seattle's minority area.[2]

Another index of the financial position of the pioneer family is the value of the housing they purchased. In seven of the eleven neighborhoods where comparison data are available, the value of the pioneer house exceeds that of the average white. In some cases there are striking differences in this respect. For example, one Negro newcomer purchased a house which he valued at $45,000, whereas the median value placed on all white housing located in the same census tract was $14,300. In another case, the comparisons were $25,000 with $13,600; $23,000 with $13,600; $36,000 with $13,600; $18,500 with $12,700. In the census tracts where the value of the Negro newcomer's housing was less than surrounding properties, the differences were not of such magnitude.

The value of homes owned by pioneers also is substantially greater than for nonwhites residing in the minority areas. The median value of these homes is $17,000, perhaps $5,000 more than the average home owned by the nonwhite resident of the minority areas. For the most part Negro pioneers purchase their homes. This is in contrast with the total nonwhite population, where over half are renters.

We examined other indices of relative economic advantage, and all point to the pioneer as a person with stable, good income, somewhat higher than his neighbors. His economic position is strikingly better than most Central Area Negroes. He is part of the Negro middle- or upper-income classes.

EDUCATION

Negroes who pioneer in neighborhood desegregation—both husbands and wives—are well educated. Half of our respondents had the B.A. or more advanced degrees. Many had attended college for a few years. In all but one census tract, the educational attainment of the Negro head of household exceeded the median school years completed by others living in the tract. A similar relationship emerged in a comparison of the newcomers with other residents interviewed in the neighborhood. In nine cases, the newcomers were equal or superior in educational attainment to *all* neighbors, close and distant. In the four other cases where comparisons were possible, the results were mixed: some neighbors were better educated, some were not. The median education for nonwhites in Seattle is 11.1 school years completed, which, of course, is less than the median of our sample of pioneers.

PRIOR INTERRACIAL EXPERIENCE

Is pioneering in neighborhood desegregation the first such experience for the Negro families in our sample, or was this the continuation of a long chain of interracial experiences? Eleven items in the interview were directed toward securing this information. A sample question was:

Can you tell me—was the immediate neighborhood you lived in as a child a segregated neighborhood? By neighborhood, we mean the block you lived on and the area right around it.

The interviewer then handed his respondent a card listing five categories: all Negro, mostly Negro, about 50-50, mostly white, all white except for one or two Negro families. The categories were read aloud together with the question:

Will you tell me which of these categories best describes the neighborhood you lived in as a child?

Similar questions probed the interracial composition of grade school, high school, college, church attended as a child, current church affiliation, parents' "best friends," own "best friends," "closest friends throughout life," and own marriage.

An *Interracial Experience Score* can be constructed by assigning one point to each answer indicating that the experiences were mostly with white persons, and zero points to each answer that indicated that the experiences were primarily with Negroes. Since there are eleven items to be considered, the score could range theoretically from zero to eleven. Such information was secured from twenty-nine different Negro respondents, sometimes taken separately from both husband and wife in the same family. The distribution of Interracial Experience Scores is shown in Table I. The actual range in scores is from zero to ten, with the median falling at four. The evidence shows that most pioneers have had extensive association with white persons prior to and current with

their present housing experiences. A few persons have had only
one or two such experiences. But with at least one third of the
sample, life experiences have been mostly with whites.

TABLE 1

INTERRACIAL EXPERIENCES OF NEGROES
WHO PIONEER IN NEIGHBORHOOD DESEGREGATION

Interracial Experience Score	Number of Negroes
0	2
1	2
2	5
3	2
4	4
5	5
6	2
7	1
8	4
9	1
10	1
	29

This interracial association is underlined by the fact that four
of our sample of twenty-four families contain white spouses: three
wives and one husband. Two other "Negroes" among these families were judged by our interviewers to be light-skinned enough
to pass for white. In addition, one Negro pioneer reported that
he had a white mother. Another had a white stepmother. Others'
parents are reported to have "passed" into the white world. The
adult children of some Negroes in our sample were also reportedly
married to whites.

It is widely believed that the possibility and the ease of interracial association is directly related to skin color, i.e., darker-
skinned Negroes are less well received by whites than are light-
skinned Negroes. For the most part, the skin color of pioneers in
this study was sufficiently dark that they usually would be considered Negroes. These findings are in direct opposition to this
myth of the importance of skin color for interracial association.

Many Negroes who pioneer in residential desegregation have a
long background in interracial living and are familiar with the

white milieux. Parallel information was not solicited from white neighbors; nor is it available for the nonwhites living in Seattle's minority areas. Thus, a comparison with them is not possible.

RELATIONS WITH THE MINORITY COMMUNITY

Pioneers are not recent newcomers to Seattle. With one exception (the Negro wife of a white man), our respondents lived elsewhere in the city before coming to the neighborhood in which they were interviewed. Six families moved to their new homes from another white area; most pioneers, however, had previously lived in the Negro area—central Seattle. Most still do business there and belong to organizations located there.

Only about a quarter of our sample of Negro families attending churches belong to those which Negroes are reported to attend most frequently in Seattle: i.e., Baptist, Methodist, Pentecostal. Most of the church-going pioneer families currently belong to predominantly white congregations. This finding again buttresses the evidence of current interracial association.

Twelve of seventeen pioneer families, for whom we have such information, reported officerships in volunteer groups and social agencies. Husbands were reported to hold sixteen officerships and wives twenty-one. Among the groups, of which these people were leaders, five were almost all-Negro; i.e., churches, NAACP, and the like. But most officerships were in the Boy Scouts, PTA, and other organizations which were predominantly white. The members of five pioneer families held no officerships. In all, pioneers are office holders much more frequently than are their white neighbors, and their leadership is exercised near-at-home, in the minority community, and in city-wide organizations.

Elsewhere in the questionnaire, five Negro respondents volunteered information about ways in which they felt they had been able to better the understanding of their neighbors on issues of prejudice and discrimination. This does not mean that the Negro newcomers purposefully became pioneers to promote better race relations. Quite the contrary, better race relations were the product of the move, rather than the cause for it. However, successful pioneering may have brought these people to the attention of both whites and Negroes and facilitated their ascent to leadership.[3]

CHAPTER FOUR

The Housing Transaction

Ours is a mobile society. Every day, in almost every neighborhood, a family moves in or moves out. Neighborhood desegregation is just a minute part of this constant succession of residents. To what extent does racial desegregation depart from normal patterns of residential succession? In this chapter findings of our study will be placed in a broader framework that describes how neighborhood machinery works in the control and integration of its members.[1]

SELECTING THE NEIGHBORHOOD

Why do people choose a particular neighborhood? White families stressed the fact that "they could afford this house," that it was a "good buy," and "that it was located near to work." Negro families with children stressed that there were good schools nearby; both stressed more spacious housing. Nearness to work did not seem to be as relevant to Negro newcomers.

Two white families purchased their homes with the hope that they would have a high resale value. Similar reasons were given by three Negro families. However, the following comments of Negro respondents show that they were more interested in protecting a major financial investment than in resale at a profit:

Our main reason for moving here was because of property values. We wanted to build a $30,000 home in an area where a home is worth that much. There are no such in the Negro areas.

Primarily we were motivated by economic consideration. We wanted to buy a house we could be sure would not depreciate in value. If we were to buy in an older area we feel this would happen. Not so if we buy in a new area, which this is. We weren't looking so much for a neighborhood, but for an *available* home. We looked all over town for available homes which we liked and this was it. To find this house, we systematically chased down all leads in all parts of Seattle before we located here.

Among both whites and Negroes, some families wanted *this*, and only *this*, neighborhood for their home. General reasons for wanting *this* neighborhood pertained to its location in the city and the quality of the housing. Some white parents wanted to assure continuity in their children's schooling. For the most part, however, families—whether white or Negro—would have been willing to buy in alternate neighborhoods if acceptable houses had been available.

FINDING THE HOUSE

In a private housing market, such as exists in Seattle as well as all over the United States, the usual source of information about properties for sale is through signs posted by owners, newspaper advertisements, or real estate agents. All of these sources were used by these Negro pioneer families.

In six of nineteen purchases, the housing was discovered through an ad or a "for sale" sign.[2] Realtors were the source in seven cases. Three houses were discovered by friends or relatives, one by a mortgage company, another through the Urban League. One Negro married the white owner. Thus, there are many ways that the Negro family learns of housing out of the ghetto. The purchase of the house involved a direct negotiation with the owner in eight cases; four houses were purchased through Negro realtors, and four through white realtors. In three cases housing was acquired through a white purchaser or builder.

Almost without exception, the pioneers in our sample were not recent newcomers to Seattle. Before moving into their present homes, nine families resided in the central city ghetto, three in interracial areas. Six families were repeaters at pioneering, since they moved from one predominantly white neighborhood to another.

THE REALTOR

With few exceptions, housing transactions are the domain of the real estate industry.[3] Customarily, people find their own housing or consult a realtor. When white residents were asked questions about this, the only community agency which helped them with housing problems was a real estate agency. One family also consulted the University of Washington Housing Bureau.

This was in marked contrast with the Negro families. None called realtors a community agency. In general they were quite vocal and detailed about the unhelpful activities of realtors. Criticisms indicated a refusal to show houses, appointments made but not kept, "lukewarm apologies" for rude behavior, and lack of diplomacy. In one case a realtor was said to have been "blunt and insulting." Even after Negroes purchased homes, some realtors continued to engage in what the newcomers called annoying behavior. One respondent reported that a realtor continually called at *his* place of business to offer him a profit for selling his new home. In another case, the realtor himself lived in the neighborhood into which the Negro family moved. Originally he was the person with whom the property was listed. He refused to sell to the Negro family, and when they had purchased the home, he helped to stir up opposition to their entry. Later he apologized to them for his part in the opposition. In a third case, a real estate firm tried to purchase the house from the owner before the Negro family could complete the paper work on an accomplished sale.

Not all the experiences of the Negro families with realtors were discriminatory. We have noted that three Negro families learned of the property they purchased through white realtors, and four completed their purchase through a white realtor. Thus, there is direct evidence of help as well as hindrance provided by white members of this profession.

It is important to distinguish between activities of individual realtors and the corporate position of the Seattle Real Estate Board. For this purpose it is necessary to introduce some current history.[4] The Seattle Real Estate Board has been vigorous in its opposition to any law preventing discrimination in housing. During the period of this study, it successfully supported a court case to void sections of the Washington State law that forbade housing discrimination. It campaigned vigorously against efforts to pass a new law. In 1962 its position was clearly stated by its executive secretary. Testifying before a special committee established by the Mayor to determine the scope of Seattle's minority housing prob-

lem, he declared that the problem was "greatly exaggerated." He
went on to state that residential segregation emerges from the
"tendency of various ethnic groups to congregate in limited
areas." "Each week," he said, "several hundred owner-advertised
homes are offered—many of which are available to any purchaser
without regard to race, color, creed or religion, and without any
third party interference or intervention." He felt that the work
of the realtor should be seen as a "professional service" rather
than a "commercial activity":

> We obviously are not contending that we are fully professional,
> but our services to clients (in housing transactions) are just as pro-
> fessional as that of a doctor, who does not operate without the
> client's permission, or the attorney, who does not file suit, regardless
> of whether the client gives permission.
> We will object to [proposed "fair housing"] legislation because it
> tends to control and dictate the very lifeblood of the work of pro-
> fessional realtors. By law, we are subjected to actions that are regu-
> lated. We can no longer serve the client. We're serving the govern-
> ment.

According to this line of reasoning, realtors believe that their
client's best interests are served by excluding Negroes or other
minorities from the neighborhood. Although he himself may de-
plore this conclusion, the realtor feels bound by his professional
code of ethics to represent his prejudiced client and implement
the values of prejudice.[5]

Evidence from the study indicates that more hostility may be
directed toward the white seller of housing than toward the Negro
buyer. This information was not sought by direct questions, but
was gained because of the open-ended nature of the interviews.
In six neighborhoods, one or more white respondents expressed
resentment against the seller, even in cases where attitudes toward
the Negro newcomers were friendly. One seller was charged with
wanting to take revenge on the neighborhood because of his
failure to secure support in rezoning the neighborhood. In another neighborhood, a respondent complained:

> He didn't say anything to anybody about selling to a Negro. This
> probably did the most to upset the neighborhood. He moved out in
> the middle of the night.

Where such a backlog of resentment may accrue to the seller, it is quite unlikely that many realtors would jeopardize their future business prospects in "home territory" by conducting such sales. On two occasions Negro pioneers reported that a white realtor attempted to negotiate for a property for them, only to have the white owner refuse the sale on racial grounds.

It would seem that hard-core segregated neighborhoods remain that way to a large extent because of an informal compact among residents not to sell to Negroes. The realtor may have initiated or nurtured this compact, but he is *not* the sole reason for its continuation. Conversely, although most white realtors are likely to support a segregated housing market, with perseverance the prospective Negro buyer can find some white (and Negro) realtors who will apply their skills to helping him acquire property in predominantly white localities.

FINANCING THE TRANSACTION

Do these Negro families experience difficulties in financing their homes? Only one made such a complaint. This respondent paid cash for his house, but did not receive the discount which he considered to be normal. One reason for this apparent lack of financial problems is the fact that our sample is made up of families with substantial incomes. A pretest study, conducted one year before this one, mentions the following incident:

> At the time the D's (Negro family) attempted to move into this neighborhood, they reported that they experienced some pressures designed to keep them out. The bank, they say, sent a letter to their landlord threatening him with loss of equity in his house if he "didn't get the D's out within two weeks," and move back into the house himself. When he was advised of this letter Dr. D paid a visit to the bank to investigate. A report on Dr. D's earnings was requested and given, whereupon the matter was dropped.[6]

This incident illustrates a difficulty which may have been more prevalent in the past, or which does not affect families with high, stable incomes, regardless of race.

COMMUNITY AGENCIES

Aside from the few families that identified realtors as a community agency, only one white family reported taking housing problems to a community agency, the University Housing Bureau. In contrast, eleven pioneer families did so. Seven asked the Urban League for help and two consulted the listings secured by the Christian Friends for Racial Equality. In the process, five complaints were filed with the Washington State Board Against Discrimination and help was requested from two other agencies— the Seattle Civic Unity Committee and the NAACP. One Negro home seeker reported regularly to the State Board any violation of the law that he noted in his search for housing.

The evidence demonstrates clearly that whites had access to channels for securing housing in Seattle which were blocked for some Negroes, who were required to turn to the specialized community agencies for service. Each Negro respondent was specifically questioned: Was help ever asked of any agency and not received? The answer was always "No." More details about agency contacts will be reported later. (See pp. 56-63.)

CHAPTER FIVE

The Neighborhood Response to Its First Pioneer Family

WHAT IS THE response of white neighborhoods to Negro entry? How does the neighborhood integration machinery work when the newcomer-stranger is a minority family? What is the outcome of this change in racial composition of the area for the newcomer and his neighbors? These are the questions which will be discussed in this chapter.

The dynamics of neighborhood change are difficult to capture through a research procedure which has involved one interview of a handful of white residents and two interviews with the Negro newcomers, plus a fragmentary analysis of population data and other records. We are dependent upon the memories and comments of our informants. To enhance the dynamic, we will report much of the story in the words of the eyewitnesses to the occasion.

THE RESPONSE TO NEGRO ENTRY

In Seattle, unlike many sections of the country, social change in the form of neighborhood integration has not been accompanied by bombings, house burnings, and expensive vandalism. Only two instances of limited physical violence were noted by our respondents, both involving fights among children.[1]

The presence of a single Negro (or interracial) family apparently is not a burning issue to the residents of the fifteen neighborhoods in our sample. Ten of the fifteen white neighbors living three blocks from the Negro newcomers had no knowledge of their presence. Seven of the fifteen white neighbors living just a block away stated that they did not know that a Negro family lived in the locality. With one exception, these respondents were not newcomers, but had been there many years. In most cases, the Negro family had also lived in the neighborhood for several years. There is no reason to believe that our informants were reluctant to provide this information to the interviewers. Instead, the inevitable conclusion is that the neighborhood communications network is effective only with near neighbors and does not encompass neighborhoods covering many blocks.

RESIDENTIAL TURNOVER—CONTINUING RESIDENTIAL STABILITY

The presence of a Negro family has not led to mass exodus of whites, nor to mass influx of Negroes. In all, our respondents named three families who were said to have moved because of the Negro entry. A few others report that they themselves intend to move some time in the future because of this, but some have held this belief for at least four years.

An estimate of residential turnover can be obtained from our sample of respondents in the fifteen neighborhoods. Fifteen of the white families moved into these neighborhoods *after* the Negroes were already residing there. The Negroes have lived in their separate neighborhoods a total of thirty-seven years, i.e., some for five years, some for four years, and so forth. A crude neighborhood turnover rate can be computed from these data. It is the ratio of the total number of years of residence by Negroes in the fifteen neighborhoods to the total number of white movers, i.e. thirty-seven to fifteen. The product is 2.5. Thus, our sample data show that two or three (2.5) white families each year move out of the fifteen neighborhoods combined, and are replaced by another two or three white families. This is a low turnover rate for Seattle neighborhoods in general.[2]

The median length of residence for pioneer families was three years as contrasted with six years for the white families. In the year between the two interviews conducted with the Negro families, two families moved. In one case, the head of the household was called to New York City to a high government post. In the other case, there was a divorce and the family broke up. One of these houses returned to white occupancy. It should also be noted that in two neighborhoods, a second Negro family moved within a few blocks of the first. One neighborhood also received several families having Chinese or Japanese ancestry.

The complete story of residential turnover is only told with a longer time perspective. However, no drastic interracial changes have occurred in the residency patterns of these neighborhoods. They have been, and continue to be, predominantly white. The presence of the Negro family has *not* proven to be an insuperable barrier to whites or Orientals moving in.

Shopping for Neighborhoods—The Initial Shock

The advent of the first Negro family usually comes as a surprise or shock to the white residents. This is almost guaranteed by the currency of myths and half truths about decline of property values and unpleasant "Negro traits." There are many social pressures for the Negro newcomer that foreshorten or completely circumvent the usual neighborhood-shopping procedures that are an adjunct to both the housing transaction and to the integration of any new family into a neighborhood.

Usually the average home buyer shops for neighborhood as well as house. The reputation, or other desirable qualities of the neighborhood, may be more important to him than the characteristics of the house he builds or buys. Frequently friends play a part in this process. They describe the locality and tell of good buys in housing. As a consequence, many newcomers know a neighborhood before they move there and have already established channels and ties which help in the absorption of the family into the social fabric of the neighborhood.

The Negro family may be severely curtailed in this shopping behavior. To be sure, the Negro home buyer is able to drive through a prospective neighborhood. He may have white friends who live there and are willing to help him in his housing search —this happened to some of the Negro families in our study. However, negative beliefs about the climate of prejudice that may exist in many places may cause this exploration to be shortened in the interests of completing a purchase when the situation is favorable. Some Negro families told of visiting a home unobtrusively before the sale, and of moving in at night before any opposition might be crystallized. White residents may have their first announcement of the new Negro family rather abruptly. They get up in the morning, look out the window, and there is the family moving into the house next door.

NEIGHBOR ATTITUDES TOWARD ENTRY

Caucasian respondents in the fifteen neighborhoods were asked to recall their feelings about the entry of the Negro newcomers with the question:

> Were your or any members of your family concerned about this when they moved in? What was your thinking?

About a third of these expressed anger, dismay, resentment; these reactions will be more fully reported in the next section on the neighborhood welcoming machinery. Another third might be classified as neutral; they replied in the following vein:

> We didn't care [about their entry]. We didn't protest, but we didn't welcome them. We weren't particularly concerned. Well, if they wanted to move in, all right, but they could keep their distance.
> We weren't worried when they moved in, but we didn't know who they were.
> It didn't matter.

On the other hand, a third of the white neighbors, expressed positive support for the event:

> We must accept anyone. We should take a religious view and love everyone the same.
> The children shouldn't be made to suffer. We're not really prejudiced.
> We lived in the house they bought. We knew it would be rough when we sold it to them. We didn't want a controversy. The strong personal conviction of my husband and I is that there shouldn't be any barriers on the basis of race or stereotyping.
> Being Jewish, we weren't prejudiced as much, and as a minority group, we were willing to see them move in.
> We didn't like her marrying a colored man, but that's her business. There wasn't anything we could do about it but accept it.
> The Negroes are an improvement over the former tenant. They are just like anyone else.
> It's a free country.

These findings again underscore the point that neighborhood desegregation is not the critical, threatening issue for most whites in Seattle that it is in some other parts of the country.

WELCOMING THE MINORITY FAMILY

There is no single neighborhood reaction to the advent of the first Negro. The social machinery for welcoming or opposing newcomers varies from neighborhood to neighborhood. In general, neither Negro nor white families living in the same neighborhoods expected official visitors during their first months of residence. Eight of the twenty-four Negro families reported such callers as contrasted with thirteen of the seventy-five white neighbors. This is probably an indication that an effort is made by some agencies and organizations to provide a special welcome for the minorities. To be sure, the white families, in general, had lived there longer than the Negro families, and perhaps had forgotten, or had less reason to remember these official visitors. In any case, the official visitors did not seem to discriminate in their calls. Most frequently they were from local churches.

Of course, the most immediate welcome or rejection of the Negro family comes from those who live nearby. Let us look at how white neighbors in three instances viewed the Negro newcomers. Negro entry is not always visible; often some neighbors who are immediately disturbed provide opposition which bubbles and seethes and presently dies out. A Caucasian widow already residing in a neighborhood married a Negro.[3] Here are comments by some of her neighbors:

> We didn't know until two months after. I had a funny feeling in the stomach. I thought this was what one might call a prejudiced feeling. I wondered why she married such a dark man and not a light-skinned Negro.
> We learned from the neighbors. They came and talked. They heard there had been a police car in the neighborhood waiting for trouble.
> Some didn't know it when we moved in. They are the quietest couple in the block. We were surprised and shocked. They are real friendly. The real estate man told my husband that a "foreign" couple lived next-door.

Specialized human relations agencies sometimes become involved at the time of entry. A second case illustrates some of the neighbors' feeling about agency intervention:

> The Negroes were insistent in getting into the neighborhood. It took over two years. They seemed to be forcing their way upon you. We didn't know who they were. We had a poor opinion of Negroes and were afraid of a bad influence on the neighborhood.
>
> Everyone was telling everyone else. One [white] man was so concerned he wanted to organize the neighbors and buy the home.
>
> Yes, we wanted to get time to find a white buyer. The owner wasn't very cooperative. . . . He had no interest in the neighborhood. He didn't care what his neighbors thought. Phone calls were made to the Housing Authority. Maybe the Real Estate Board was called and the NAACP and the Urban League. The callers were told they could get no help from them.
>
> The Urban League wants to salt and pepper the neighborhood.

In the third instance there was no surprise, since the Jones family was known to be building its own home in the white neighborhood. Some comments of the five white neighbors follow:

> There was some talk about getting a petition up, but I never saw a petition or learned whether one had actually been circulated. It didn't disturb us [about their moving here]. We didn't have any feelings about it one way or the other. We were not concerned. We didn't plan to associate with them so we let them live their life, and we are going to live ours.
>
> The next-door neighbor made a fuss about it. He's a police officer who is very racial minded. He didn't even want his child to talk to them. He cursed and carried on for several days.
>
> Some neighbors were hostile, would sing "Old Black Joe." Others poured paint on a portion of their home while it was being built. Someone drove a car across their new lawn. I don't approve of these things.
>
> We were plenty upset. But they have the nicest home in the neighborhood. They are nice, quiet people—better than most whites.
>
> They were here when we came. It didn't make any difference to us. We heard that some families were upset by it. We've never heard anything since we've lived here. I guess the trouble was over before we arrived.

Church and School Visits

Although churches frequently are the first to greet the new Negro families, other organizations gradually extend a welcoming hand. Only seven of the twenty-four cases for which we have information report that they were *not* visited at home with an invitation to participate in a neighborhood activity or organization, and two of these families had lived in their neighborhoods only a few weeks. Others reported that they were seldom at home during the usual times for visiting.

The presence of children in a family helps to establish ties in a neighborhood, both alliances and conflicts. Comments, such as the following, were found in almost every neighborhood:

> We have two or three sets of neighbors and they are nice. They have kids and they are over here all the time. [Negro respondent]
>
> We had a birthday party, all girls. Everyone who was invited came. We have become friendly. It was a mixed party. [Negro respondent]
>
> Our kids are not on speaking terms. The people in back [Negro] have five children who are noisy and run through our house. They also had a cat which came in our house. Finally, I gave the cat away. Now we are not on speaking terms. [White respondent]
>
> Our children are older now but when they were smaller they brought us closer to the neighbors who had children of the same age. . . . The longer we have lived here, the friendlier we have become. [White respondent]
>
> Arguments come up and there is more friction as we get to know each other. We don't have any trouble. People know each other and develop likes and dislikes. We have two children now who involve us in the neighborhood. However, we never get to see the people who work. [White respondent]

It is logical with this common interest in children that new Negro families are invited to join the PTA and scouting activities centered in the schools. Next to churches, these organizations are most frequently mentioned by Negro families as having extended to them an invitation to participate. Such visits in many cases led Negro families to join local churches and organizations.

JOINING LOCAL ORGANIZATIONS—THE NEIGHBORHOOD INTEGRATION PROCESS

In the process of becoming established in a neighborhood, are there differences among Negroes and whites in their membership affiliations? First, it should be noted that Negro families report more memberships in local neighborhood organizations than their white neighbors. Negroes interviewed have a total of twenty memberships in eight neighborhoods. In contrast, thirty of the seventy-five white families account for fifty-seven memberships in fourteen neighborhood clubs. Active white families have about two memberships per family as compared with about three memberships per family for the active Negro newcomers.

Neighborhoods differ in the amount or tempo of organizational life. A *Total Activity Score* was computed for each neighborhood, separately, to assess this factor. In twelve of fifteen neighborhoods, Negro families were as active or more active than their white neighbors in local organizations.

The Total Activity Score was derived from the total number of memberships of residents in locally based organizations. An additional point was entered into the score for each affirmative answer to the following question:

> Is this the kind of neighborhood in which neighbors visit each other frequently?

The Total Activity Scores for the neighborhoods ranged from one through nineteen. Neighborhoods then were grouped into three classes: inactive, moderately active, and very active. Inactive neighborhoods scored six points or less on the Total Activity Score, and frequently were characterized by the respondents as "having no such organization," or as being "unfriendly." Moderately active neighborhoods scored from eight through fifteen on the Total Activity Scores. Most residents belonged to one or two neighborhood groups. The one very active neighborhood scored nineteen on the Total Activity Score, or about three memberships per resident. This neighborhood had both an active "social club" and a community council. Seven neighborhoods, thus, were classified as "inactive," seven as "moderately active," and one as "very active."

In all but three neighborhoods, Negro families equaled or exceeded their white neighbors in neighborhood involvement. The three neighborhoods with less Negro participation deserve further analysis.

One neighborhood was rated as "inactive" with a single white resident belonging to the PTA and another to a local church. This is the neighborhood, mentioned earlier, where the Jones family built their home. Although the initially hostile reaction to their entry has worn off somewhat, apparently there is an aftermath. One neighbor said: "They don't push themselves into friendship." Another remarked: "I felt they were hurt, feeling that the neighborhood would not accept them more readily. They found out they weren't being accepted. They are quiet." A third neighbor commented: "I let my children play with them and everyone got down on me with looks and remarks. I put a stop to that. It's so hard to please everyone!" The Negro mother tells this story of her child:

> He came home and asked us why a friend treated him differently than his white friends? He said he wanted to be the color of his mother rather than his father, that is, he wanted to be light skinned, like me. I told him one color was as nice as the next and we need all kinds. The children talk about this at school. They reflect the attitudes of their parents. I think my boy gets along. He knows where he isn't welcome.

Her husband tells this story:

> People are friendlier than when we moved in. A new neighbor invited us over for dinner and we did the same. They are a young couple, 19 and 23. The couple said they lost the friendship of another neighbor because of drinking coffee with us.

Thus, the aftermath of bitter feelings persists. In this case, however, it would seem that the differences in neighborhood involvement between the Negro newcomers and their white neighbors are not marked.

In two "moderately active" neighborhoods, the Negro families have no local organizational affiliations. In both neighborhoods there had been active campaigns to prevent their entry. Later, after the move-in, official callers invited their participation in the church and PTA.

In one instance, however, the wife responded on the following Sunday by attending the morning Mass, only to receive a frosty reception. She never returned to the church. Three of her neighbors, who resented the family's use of social agencies to "crash" the neighborhood, now make the almost identical reply:

> They were willing to take any house to get into the neighborhood. But they're not sociable. We're not sociable . . . no social contact. Why should they force themselves on us? They're probably

in their fifties. Good people in general! They haven't bothered anybody.

In the second neighborhood, the Negro family reported:

Things have relaxed quite a bit. Some things have not changed. It is up to the individual. One new neighbor waved as he passed by. Another invited us to an open house. The one, who didn't like our children hasn't changed a bit. Maybe we are getting used to it.

The white neighbors' comments, in general, are positive and friendly:

They are polite, although they stay to themselves. Their children stay in their yard. . . . They dress well . . . keep the house neat. Fine as if they were white!

The interracial barriers come down slowly. In the first neighborhood, one white lady reported of her neighbor: "They are equal to anyone in the neighborhood—I met her at a PTA Christmas party." In the other neighborhood, one wife reported:

My husband insisted on inviting the ————'s to our open house, or otherwise there wouldn't have been one. That poor man! After that open house his hands were soaking with fear that things wouldn't go well! We think they are very fine people.

From the comments above, it appears that, although desegregation is occurring in the smaller neighborhood circle, it has not yet been reflected in local organizational memberships for the Negro families. To be sure, in each case there are other factors than race relations at work. In both instances the Negro families indicated that they were personally too busy to become involved in such organizations.

NEIGHBORHOOD ORGANIZATION AS A CHANNEL FOR DESEGREGATION

Desegregation has proceeded more rapidly in neighborhood institutional facilities, school and church, than it has in noninstitutionalized local voluntary membership groups.

Table 2 lists the reported memberships of active families in the fifteen neighborhoods. For both Negroes and whites, the church and PTA are most frequently mentioned. However, twelve white families (21 per cent) reported affiliations with neighborhood improvement and social clubs as compared with one Negro family (5 per cent). This difference may be more apparent than real, since one neighborhood accounts for four memberships in the social club by whites and five memberships in the community improvement club, including four white families and the Negro family. However, there are many comments scattered through the interviews with white neighbors indicating that social clubs and "coffee-klatches" helped to originate some of the petitions opposing Negro entry; that some community improvement associations became the center for efforts to buy back the pioneers' homes. These efforts seldom escape the attention of the Negro family, as, for example, in two instances where the improvement club made direct bids to buy the Negro newcomer's home.

TABLE 2

COMPARISON OF NEGROES AND WHITES
IN TYPES OF ORGANIZATIONAL MEMBERSHIPS

Type of Organization	Percentage of Total Reported Memberships	
	Negro (N*=20)	White (N*=56)
Church	40%	41%
Church-related clubs	10	5
Parent Teacher Association	20	23
Scouting organizations	15	3
Community improvement club	5	12
Neighborhood social club	—	9
Political organizations	—	5
Fraternal	5	2
Other	5	—

* N=total number of memberships.

Obviously such efforts are not likely to win future support from the Negro newcomer; furthermore, the issue is divisive. There are many attitudes toward racial and religious segregation. The conflict that is engendered in such a campaign may cause the community club to lose the support of the entire neighborhood. Even the best organized of the campaigns against Negro entry eventually passed over, so far as we were able to determine in this study—with one exception.

CHAPTER SIX

The Neighborhood Integration Process

PRECEDING chapters have dealt with the neighborhood response to the entry of the first pioneer family. In this section these activities will be woven into a theory of how the process of neighborhood integration comes about.[1]

The following four stages can be identified: (1) pre-entry, (2) entry, (3) accommodation, (4) integration. In identifying these four stages there is no inference that each is prerequisite to the next, nor that every newcomer will inevitably pass through all of the stages in that order until integration occurs.

PRE-ENTRY

To be sure, pre-entry is always the beginning stage in the neighborhood integration process. One aspect of this involves the newcomer. His act of purchasing or building a house represents an initial investment in the area. Shopping for neighborhoods has been discussed more fully in chapter four. The second aspect involves neighborhood awareness. The knowledge that a Negro family is about to move in may set off a favorable or an unfavorable neighborhood reaction.

There is much debate about whether such advance notice increases or decreases resistance to minority newcomers.[2] Using our data, a test of this question could be made in twelve neigborhoods.[3] In the seven neighborhoods where there were "warnings," opposition developed in three; two apparently were unconcerned, and in two others the usual "friendly" welcome was extended to the newcomers where, without too much delay, they received visitors and invitations to join local organizations. The nature of the opposition is described in the vignettes on the Reed family and the Jones family. It will be recalled that the Reeds were introduced to the neighborhood at a tea given by the previous owners of the house. They were welcomed by the immediate neighbors, and this cordial welcome prevailed at the time of the interview, although in the larger neighborhood there was continuing hostility toward them and toward the sellers of the housing, who were still residents in the area. In the latter case, the Jones family built their own home, and so their presence in the neighborhood was known long before they moved in. The active hostility they encountered simmered down, but still remained after three years.

Of the five neighborhoods that received no warning, one was "friendly" as described in the vignette about the Parsons family; two might be described as "neutral," as represented in the vignette of the Price family; and two were hostile.

The neighborhood into which the Strong family moved received no warning, but engendered much hostility to the minority newcomers, at least until the principal antagonists departed. The fifth unwarned neighborhood had a mixed response, but the pioneer family pointedly reported that they were *not* invited and "*not* welcome" in local neighborhood groups even after three years of residence there. Does prior notice impede integration? Apparently there is no universal pattern that applies to all neighborhoods. Further observation and experimentation is needed before fixed conclusions can be reached.

ENTRY

The second stage in the process of neighborhood integration obviously comes with the advent of the pioneer family. The neighbors are not always immediately aware of such entry. We have seen that most persons living three blocks away and many living just one block away from the residence of the Negro newcomers were not even aware of their presence after they had lived for some time in the area. In some cases, as with interracial marriage, the next-door neighbor may not discover the event till months after it occurs. It is possible that many "Negroes" are so light-skinned and uncommunicative that their presence is unknown to those living alongside.

The flurry of open opposition occurs during the move-in and the brief period after it, if at all. If the neighbors have been opposed to the move-in, they may feel thwarted by the Negro entry and take part in some act of spite or petty vandalism, or they may attempt to circulate a petition to buy out the newcomer. Those neighbors who feel most strongly may move out, but such departures seem to be the exception rather than the rule. In the neighborhoods studied, the crisis of the entry stage seemed to end within a few weeks.

The effect of announcement before the arrival of the Negro newcomers was discussed in the last section. But there also can be a warning in another way. Will white families buy homes in a neighborhood containing one Negro family? Quite obviously, the answer is yes, for there were fifteen respondents in the sample who did so. But did they know of the presence of the Negro family when they purchased? Were they warned of this before they completed their housing transactions? If so, what was the effect of such a warning on their subsequent integration into the neighborhood?

Of the fifteen latest white newcomers, eight knew of the Negro family living there when they purchased their homes, most often because they were told this by the former owner. Such sentiments were expressed as:

> We have no strong prejudiced feeling.
> At first it bothered us. But we asked around the neighborhood and they told us that the Negro family were the nicest people, so we moved in.
> I'm not prejudiced against nobody . . . I wanted the house I bought. I don't care what's beside me as long as they keep in their place.

Two white newcomers in one neighborhood were alerted to the availability of housing by the Negro family living there.

Among the white families who discovered their Negro neighbor after the purchase, these are some typical comments:

> The real estate agent told my husband that a foreign couple lived next door. We were surprised and shocked when we found out they were Negroes. But they are the quietest family on the block.

> We bought because of the house, not because of the neighbors. We don't know them, and they don't know us.
>
> We didn't know our neighbor was a Negro until we moved in. We bought here because it was so cheap. The owner said he was anxious to sell. We have had friends of different races. We lived in an all-Negro project in Port Orchard. Even though they asked us to move out of the project, we didn't. We had a wonderful experience. When we knew our neighbors were Negro, we went over. Two days later we were playing ping-pong with them.

Evidently, the presence of one Negro family does not destroy the desirable housing and neighborhood characteristics for most whites, and for some it is a distinct asset.

Ironically, the presence of a Negro family may actually help to create and consolidate neighborhood bonds that would not have come into being without their presence. In some cases, the family may become the focus of neighborhood attention, a "problem" or an "opportunity" the neighborhood has in common. Networks of organization and beliefs that never existed before may appear in the neighborhood. These social networks may not facilitate the entry of the Negro, but they may turn a relatively unorganized group of residents into a set of acting groups with common purposes.

Of special interest to the subject at hand are the two white newcomers who were aided in their search for housing by the Negro resident in the neighborhood. Both spoke of the pioneer as being a personal friend and an associate at work. In this case, the friendship (i.e., integration) existed before neighboring, and the integration stage came prior to the entry stage. Similarly, the graphic comment of the white neighbor, who was surprised and happy to find himself living alongside a Negro family in his newly purchased home, indicates that he saw this as facilitating his own integration into the neighborhood. He felt that the Negro family would have interests and attitudes similar to his own, and he was right—"Two days later," he reported, "we were playing ping-pong with them."

ACCOMMODATION

Welcoming newcomers in private residential areas is a traditional form of neighborliness. This has become institutionalized

in some schools and churches. It is a form of accommodation.*
But once the courtesy is performed, it need not be repeated. Consequently, the friendly welcome is just the beginning of accommodation. Neighborhoods vary in their welcoming apparatus, but
apparently the pioneer families in our sample received the same
treatment as others in their particular locality.

A second level of accommodation involves neighborly interac-
tions of a rather necessary sort. For example, perhaps the postman
leaves a package for the person next door; an emergency occurs in
which assistance is rendered; children get into fights and must be
separated; a ball is batted into a neighbor's yard; a cup of sugar
is needed desperately. These are the little events that accompany
acceptance of the minority family and may lead to integration in
the neighborhood.

Anecdotes by the respondents illustrate such accommodation.
Mr. Parsons' comments are typical:

> The neighbor's dog got in my yard and couldn't get out. I could
> have helped, but instead I waited until he was forced to come over
> to get him. He had never spoken to us before this. This seemed to
> "break the ice." Now we get along very well.

Some pioneers report taking the initiative:

> If I see that a neighbor needs help with his car, I'm right there
> to help him. If someone else is sick, I'm over to mow his lawn.
> We picked up the neighbor's spastic child when he fell in the
> road near our garage. After this they became very friendly to us,
> waving and so forth. [The parents of the spastic child had been
> leaders of opposition to the Negro family.]

In ten of the fifteen neighborhoods such examples of mutually necessary help are mentioned. These do not always progress to further
intimacy. One pioneer and his neighbor together hired a bull-
dozer to level their yards, but this did not lead to further neighboring. In fact, the Negro family feels that friendly relations with
this white family have declined.

---

* The term accommodation refers to a state of equilibrium between individuals or groups in which certain working arrangements have been agreed
upon or accepted. Thus, the individuals or groups in question have come to
know what to expect of one another. Accommodation may range from
friendly situations to hostile ones.

INTEGRATION

It is fiction to talk of complete acceptance or complete rejection of a family by a neighborhood, since apparently a large proportion of the residents—perhaps the majority—are not too concerned about the collective life of the neighborhood. They may become concerned when their property investment is threatened. Since this has not been the case in the examples of pioneering reported in this study, there has been no reason for active neighborhood involvement by these relatively passive residents.

To what extent has integration occurred in the fifteen neighborhoods that make up the central focus of the study? One index of integration was provided by questions about neighborhood acceptance of the newcomers.

All respondents who knew of the presence of the Negro family were asked how they felt about having them as neighbors. One replied that he was "very unhappy" about this; four were "unhappy." In contrast, twenty-three persons said they felt "very happy" or "happy" about this. The balance of the sixty families providing such information were "neutral."

In addition to giving their own opinions on the subject, they were asked to indicate how their neighbors felt about having Negroes in the neighborhood. In most cases, neighborhood acceptance of the Negro newcomers was seen to be about the same as the respondents' own acceptance. However, twenty persons, one third of the respondents, indicated that they themselves were happier about having Negro neighbors than others living about them. This finding will be discussed more fully later. For the present, it is sufficient to note that the Negro pioneer families are reported to be accepted both by the respondent and his neighbors in the vast majority of cases. In the detailed examination of neighborhoods which follows, it will be seen that in some areas there has been accommodation and in others integration.

Acceptance at the level of friendly accommodation seems to be the case in the neighborhood in which the Price family are renters, as illustrated in these comments of three white neighbors:

> They seem nice and clean, quiet and young. They have two kids, twelve and eight. I think they're out of school. I think he probably

has an education. They're not rich. The kids mix. I think they go out of their way not to interfere, but they're not antisocial.

The boys are well mannered. So are the parents. They're quiet. The boys are very nice and have been in the yard. They seem to mix well with other children. They are an improvement over the prior family. They keep things up and are more quiet than the prior family.

Both work, and I think he goes to school. I haven't talked to them yet [in five months]. They seem O.K. They are nice people. They keep their home up.

Acceptance at the level of integration seems to be the case in the neighborhood in which the Johns purchased their home. The comments by all of their next-door neighbors indicate that the John family is considered as ideal. These people knew that a Negro family lived in the area when they purchased their homes. They were prepared in advance. Interviews with Mr. John and all three of his nearest neighbors indicate that visiting in each other's homes occurs several times weekly. The Johns obviously are accepted by their immediate neighbors, although as the comments will show, this acceptance may not extend to other Negro families. Note how Mrs. John is identified as Puerto Rican by one neighbor, and as Hawaiian by another. She did in fact grow up in Hawaii. Nevertheless, it appears that accommodation has become integration for this pioneer family.

They are the best people in the neighborhood. They have the best behaved children. Mrs. John has a great interest in her children. She's a wonderful mother. They don't go out a lot. I don't think they want to push themselves on others. They wait until people come to see them, and they do because they like them so much. When we moved here, Mrs. John came over and was so friendly. She was a great help when I was expecting the baby and after he was born. They are really neat people, always working around their yard, and she is an immaculate housekeeper. I hope they never move away!

She is Puerto Rican and he is very light skinned. They are not regular Negroes. We wouldn't want lower class Negroes living here, but these people are real nice. They're both educated and active in the church. Mr. John is active in a lot of things. She doesn't get out much because of her children. They are very friendly, but not overly so. When we moved in they were very helpful. When I was remodeling, I ran my hand through the glass and he rushed me to the hospital. They took care of my son and called my wife.

He is a lawyer. They are exceptionally fine people, the most cultured people in the neighborhood. You couldn't meet finer people anywhere. He is very active in many things. They have high principles, kind of above the rest of us actually.

Of the fifteen neighborhoods in the sample, fourteen could be rated according to the stage of integration they had achieved. In only four were the Negro newcomers integrated into the immediate next-door neighbors' social system; and even in these cases there was no evidence of integration spreading outward to the larger neighborhood, where, for the most part, their presence was unknown. In the other ten areas there were varying levels of accommodation—from suspended hostility to relative unconcern. Length of residence seems to be associated with level of integration. The pioneers had lived in the four most integrated areas for five, five, four, and two years respectively. However, length of residence by itself is not sufficient to bring about integration. For example, the Strong family, which continues to experience suspended hostility, has lived in the same neighborhood for almost four years.

The friendliness extended by whites to Negro next-door neighbors does not necessarily lead to a general endorsement of housing desegregation or interracial brotherhood. This was illustrated in the comments above by white neighbors who were enthusiastic about the John family, but not about "lower-class Negroes." Altogether, about one third of the fifty white respondents in the sample expressed fears about the influx into their neighborhoods of more Negro families, even though they were asked no question specifically on this topic.

Does living next-door to a Negro family, in and of itself, bring about tolerance and friendship? [4] Next-door neighbors were compared with more distant neighbors in their answer to the question:

In general, how do you feel about having the colored family as neighbors?

The respondent indicated his feelings on a five-point rating scale from "very friendly" through "very unfriendly," with the interviewer instructed to repeat the respondent's selection to him, asking for confirmation. In two neighborhoods, the close neighbors were more friendly than the distant neighbors; in six cases the reverse was true; in one case the ratings were about the same. An examination of the total interview indicated that the ratings were consistent with opinions expressed by each neighbor in response to other questions relevant to neighboring. Therefore, it appears that nearness, in and of itself, is not a sufficient condition for friendliness or hostility.

The dynamics of neighborhood integration are worthy of more detailed study than was possible in this examination of little clusters of six residents living in the same geographical areas. From this start, however, it can be concluded that neighborhood desegregation through pioneering is feasible, and that in most cases it leads to successful accommodation and sometimes integration of a particular Negro family in its small next-door-neighbors social system.[5] We will now turn to an examination of how social agencies become involved in this desegregation process.

CHAPTER SEVEN

The Activities of the Antidiscrimination Network

SCATTERED through the previous chapters have been references to specialized community agencies which have been established to work on problems of intergroup relations. These agencies are sometimes called the "antidiscrimination network."

Of what help are these agencies in the pioneering process? How are they seen by the white residents living where the Negro moves? What do the citizenry believe are the proper functions of these agencies? What is the invisible agenda of these human relations organizations, if any? These are the questions with which we will deal in this chapter.[1]

FEELINGS ABOUT SOCIAL AGENCIES

Toward the end of the interview, each respondent was given a long list of community agencies and asked whether any had been involved "in the neighborhood affairs concerning the colored family." In five localities, whites said that one or more agencies were involved: the number in the parentheses below indicates the frequency with which the agency was identified. They were: Urban League (4), police (4), State Board Against Discrimination (3), Civic Unity Committee (2), NAACP (2), Real Estate Board or agent (2), church (1), American Civil Liberties Union (1), American Jewish Committee (1).

Two points should be made about the selections: first, agencies were reported by whites to be involved in only *four* neighborhoods of the fifteen in the sample. Negro respondents, however, stated that they received help from these community agencies in *eight* neighborhoods.[2]

Second, white neighbors made little or no mention of the activities of strictly local organizations, such as churches, schools, scouting groups, and community clubs, all of which were identified on the list of community agencies given the respondent. Eleven of the Negro families reported official visitors from eighteen different local organizations, usually the church or the PTA. Thus, much of the work of Seattle agencies and organizations seems to be unobtrusive or unseen to anyone other than the principal recipients. The negative comments noted below are reserved by the white residents (at least) for the network of specialized city-wide human relations agencies, rather than for community agencies in general or local organizations in particular. This will have important implications for a program of amelioration, to be discussed later in this study.

Following the checklist of community agencies, neighbors were asked to rate how they felt about agency activities. The ratings for all neighbors were: very favorable (2), favorable (9), neutral (29), unfavorable (11), very unfavorable (4), no comment (20). Most near neighbors claimed to be "neutral." When they were not "neutral," they were more often "favorable" than "unfavorable." Neighbors living further away more often were "unfavorable" or had no comment. For the total group, attitudes were preponderantly negative. It became evident that when comments accompanying the rating scale were analyzed, favorable attitudes were usually qualified. Neighbors favored agencies helping:

(1) if help is *necessary:* "They might serve to ease conflict and physical violence";
(2) if help is *discreet:* "Depends on how they do it. They shouldn't arouse attention. No use advertising it";
(3) if help is *effective:* "It must be handled effectively." "Depends on the staff";
(4) if Negro is *worthy:* "As long as they stay in their place, I don't mind. They should be checked out to see if they're a bunch of trash";
(5) if the problem is *remote:* "As long as they are not in my area, I don't care if they get help."

The neutral comments were similar in tone; some examples are:

It serves a purpose for those who need it. If it helps them out. I think they have a nerve keeping people out.

I don't think it would alter the situation. Not necessary. The church would be OK. I don't know what they could do.

I don't feel they have a place in this. It shoud be up to the individual neighborhood. As long as the colored family minds their own business, there is no reason to bother them. People should keep within their own race. Organizations should not help people move in. I don't think they can do much about keeping Negroes out. I prefer not to have a colored family in the neighborhood.

The unfavorable attitudes indicated that agency intervention might do more harm than good, that agencies should not "tell people what to do," and that agencies are not very effective. The most unfavorable comments were outspoken "against Negroes" and "against being pushed."

Only one forthright favorable attitude toward agencies was expressed:

I think the NAACP and the Anti-Defamation League can do a big job when discrimination is a problem. The ADL helps Jewish families a lot. The Urban League is active and does a lot for Negroes. They are useful when trouble arises about discrimination. Those groups are important.

The negative comments about the city-wide human relations agencies were also shared by the Negro newcomers. They were asked to rate their contacts with the list of community agencies as "helpful" or "not helpful" and to give reasons. Many families declined to comment. In all, only three of the twenty-four Negro families asked this question rated the service as helpful. Some typical answers were:

I couldn't get any help. They just referred me to another agency —just passing the buck.

It is helpful, but don't know exactly where it would be helpful. It is part of their business.

I feel that agencies interfering doesn't help—it inflames. You've got to do it on your own. Publicity and excitement just gets attitudes riled up.

They referred us to only *one* real estate agent and he was not interested.

They were as helpful as they *could* be. . . .

In contrast, friendly help from neighborhood organizations was appreciated, as expressed in comments such as:

> The principal of the school came to our house and shook our hands. This helped (with the neighbor's attitudes towards us).

How Can Agency Services Be Improved?

Nineteen Negro respondents commented. Eight indicated lack of familiarity with agencies or expressed pessimism about their potential to do much:

> These agencies can't seek homes.
> They could have a housing agency, but real estate won't stand for that. . . .

Eleven persons urged broad educational campaigns to clear up the misconceptions of the prejudiced, or to "help Negro people be proud of their race and not to be angry about it." They admonished realtors to sell to anyone who could afford to buy, without "jacking up the price for Negro minorities." The Urban League and the State Board Against Discrimination were urged to "Let the public know more clearly their functions, or what they can do and cannot do. What they do is a mystery to many." When the Negro newcomer was asked if there was anything the agencies could have done that would have been helpful in his own particular case, nine persons had no comment. Four others stated they "really didn't need any help," or "feel it's an individual problem." Six favored neighborhood education measures ranging from a "government canvass" to "talking to people." Churches and unions were suggested as being particularly effective in such efforts. Six other comments reiterated the call for effective pressure on real estate agents and for more efficient listing services. One mentioned that such listing services require specialized knowledge to deal with the subject.

White neighbors were asked if there was anything that agencies might do "that would be effective in relieving tensions or conflicts that might occur." Fifty-two persons said "no," adding such comments as:

> I don't think they could really solve any problems.
> It's human nature.

This is a question between neighbor and neighbor.

People themselves work it out. The more organizations involved, the more people get riled up. Probably the South would not be the way it is if it were not for the newspapers.

We need an organization for the equal rights of white people.

They (Negroes) are pushing too much. It's unreasonable.

Twelve white neighbors, including two who thought social agencies could do nothing, suggested that "perhaps education might help." One person favored working with churches and children, adding, "They can mold young minds, but not the minds of older people." Seven persons advocated intervention by a social agency only "if there is trouble," but comments again reflected pessimism:

> If there were trouble, they could talk to people and reason with them. Education might help, but I don't think agencies can do much. Prejudice isn't reasonable.
>
> Nothing can be done—unless to stop a fight. You can't change a person's feeling.

Less Visible Activities of the Antidiscrimination Network

In the comments of the Negro newcomers and their white neighbors, there were several references to activities of agencies, such as the Urban League, Civic Unity Committee, the State Board Against Discrimination, Christian Friends for Racial Equality, ADL, NAACP, and others. These are among the best known of the organizations making up Seattle's antidiscrimination network, all having been in existence for over a decade.

We also noted that in four neighborhoods, where Negro newcomers received "help," five white neighbors were not aware of it, even those living next door. This suggests that such work may be unpublicized and unobtrusive. Possibly agency help is most successful where it is unknown, except to a few people.

One way to estimate the amount of invisible help was through a systematic content analysis of the official minutes of these agencies.[3] The minutes were assessed to discover the number of inches of space devoted, first, to any form of housing activity; and second, to the range of housing activities. Although the number of years of available minutes vary by agency, and there are other short-

TABLE 3

FREQUENCY OF INTERGROUP CONTACTS ON MINORITY HOUSING AND
NEIGHBORHOOD DESEGREGATION AMONG HUMAN RELATIONS
AGENCIES AND OTHER GROUPS

Desegregation	Among 8 Human Relations Agencies	With All Other Community Groups
Totals	126	258
1. In white neighborhoods: help entry of minorities; find sellers; crisis management in early stages	23	38
2. In white neighborhoods: help integration after entry of minorities	4	10
3. In public housing: help secure interracial policies, or more public housing	8	7
4. Of public accommodations	15	12
Housing and Urban Renewal		
5. Top policy making	0	2
6. Relocation of minority families in clearance programs	4	11
7. To promote citizen participation in integration within neighborhoods	18	3
8. To facilitate building of interracial housing	7	19
Education on Minority Housing Problem		
9. With general public	12	39
10. With special groups, such as high school children, realtors	4	29
11. Of influential community leaders	2	11
Legislation, Organization, Research		
12. Efforts to secure passage of fair-housing legislation	14	24
13. Efforts to help human relations groups to organize and run effectively	5	16
14. Research on minority housing and desegregation	1	9
15. Other, nature of contact unknown	9	28

comings in these materials as a source of data, we can derive a rough approximation relevant to the purposes of the analysis.

First, the tabulation indicated that housing occupied only about 10 per cent of the space in the minutes of all agencies combined—it has not been the most stressed activity of these agencies. Furthermore, this proportion varied little in the minutes of the two agencies which spanned the period, 1950-56, as compared with the minutes of five agencies spanning 1957-61.[4]

Table 3 shows the results of the second phase of the analysis. Note that the first column of numbers refers to all intergroup contacts among the eight leading human relations agencies in the city. Included are the six mentioned in the paragraphs above, plus the Greater Seattle Housing Council and the King County Inter-group Relations Council.[5] The second column of numbers refers to intergroup contacts between all community groups and the five organizations for which we had the official minutes.

The most frequent subject of intergroup contact is item 1, which is directly concerned with help given to first minority newcomers in residential desegregation, closely followed by education of the general public about minority housing problems (item 9) and legislative campaigns to secure the passage of fair-housing legislation (item 12). This analysis of the minutes, therefore, supports the conclusions arrived at from our primary data. Human relations agencies are concerned about help to first Negro residents, although in the total activity of each of the five major agencies, efforts directed at housing desegregation consume only about 1 or 2 per cent of their working time.

It well might be asked why organizations in the antidiscrimination network have *not* provided more active and aggressive help for first Negro residents in neighborhood desegregation.[6] There are probably three reasons for this: First, our sample shows that many neighborhoods are ready to receive their first Negro residents with a minimum of stress and strain. The pioneer can be successful by himself, especially if he is resourceful and has the financial means. In such a case, community agencies learn about the move after it has been made, and unless there is a crisis they may not be called upon for aid. In two cases in our sample, where the Washington State Board Against Discrimination sent its staff to investigate a crisis, the precipitating incidents passed over so rapidly that it was not necessary to file formal actions under the then-existing law.

The specialized human relations agencies may also be reluctant to take direct, positive action in pioneering because there is a lack of certain knowledge about the most helpful strategy. Lacking this certain knowledge, agency practitioners often vacillate between alternative courses of action.

A third reason may pertain to the effectiveness of pioneering as a solution to the minority housing problem. With the limited resources that are available to human relations agencies, and the many calls that are made on them for service, perhaps—deliberately or not deliberately—the organizational decision is made to concentrate on those programs which they believe are likely to have the greatest impact on residential segregation.

Seattle Civic Unity, for example, has emphasized educational programs directed toward the white majority, whose prejudice is seen to be the root of racial discrimination. On the other hand, many agencies direct their work toward amelioration of social conditions for the large Negro population living in the Central Area, rather than toward the few who are able to leave this area.

CHAPTER EIGHT

Conclusions
Program for Action Now

WHAT DOES this study add to our knowledge of neighborhood desegregation? The purpose of this chapter will be to summarize briefly the results of the analysis and to relate these to current knowledge of the subject.

SOME MYTHS ABOUT RACE AND HOUSING ARE REFUTED

There are many myths and half-truths about the course and consequences of Negro entry into formerly all-white neighborhoods. These myths and half-truths have helped to maintain segregation and discrimination.[1] One of the major findings of this study is to discount the universality of these myths, in particular those concerning the decline of neighborhood property values, white escape from Negro invasion, the inevitability of violence, and the impossibility of neighborhood desegregation and integration.

Property values do not collapse

It is frequently held that property values decline following Negro entry, despite the many valid studies which deny or modify this blanket statement.[2] Questions about this problem were asked only of those white residents, some fifty in number, who were aware that a Negro family had moved into their neighborhoods. Forty of these felt that there had been no decline in property values. Of the ten residents who expressed another opinion, only one cited a specific—i.e., his parents lowered the rent on an apartment to get a tenant following the move-in of the Negro. Five respondents of this latter group stated they did not know what had happened to property values. The neighbors were all but unanimous in their belief that property maintenance by the Negro family was at or above par for the neighborhood.

The new Negro families were also asked questions about property values. Of the nineteen providing such information, one believed there had been a decline in neighborhood property values. With this exception, all said that values had risen. Earlier in this report we noted that the Negro pioneer sees his purchase of a home as a large investment, which he wishes to protect. This is one reason for location out of the ghetto. Much evidence was offered by Negroes and whites alike as to improvements made in the housing and grounds of newly-acquired property.

Neighborhood racial composition remains stable

Studies of the large central cities have often shown that there is succession of one ethnic group after another as residents of a particular geographical area. In the past it was believed that no group would replace Negroes once they had become residents of an area. This iron law of racial succession has been challenged during the past decade by contrary evidence. In the East, for example, the most recent immigrant group to New York City and Newark, New Jersey—white and Negro Puerto Ricans—has gradually replaced the former native Negro population.[3] Urban renewal projects by deliberate plan have cleared entire areas in many cities of their Negro and minority populations, replacing the slums with expensive apartment buildings and white residents.[4] Thus, even in the central city, the so-called inevitable process of succession has been altered.

Our study is about predominantly white neighborhoods, especially the areas at the outskirts of the city and its suburbs. What has happened to the fifteen neighborhoods about which we have information dating back for ten years or more? We interviewed most Negro families twice, each interview one year apart. In two neighborhoods there was evidence that one or two other minority families had moved into the immediate area in the recent past.

In most instances, the first Negro family remained the only Negro family. Thus, flooding is not an inevitable consequence in this setting. In most of the neighborhoods we interviewed some white residents who had moved there *after* the Negro entry. The stability of an area seems to be based on a complex of factors, and not solely on the race of one family. Our study, then, disproves the inevitability of racial succession.

Integration can occur without violence

Newspaper accounts of neighborhood desegregation too often emphasize the sensational. Bombings and violence usually warrant reportage, and once in a while there is a story of how a neighborhood resisted blockbusting, or welcomed a minority family.[5] In our sample of neighborhoods, the process was much less dramatic. There was little violence and vandalism. Most neighborhoods have accepted their first Negro family without much stress and strain. This finding is not at variance with similar studies made in Pittsburgh,[6] Kalamazoo,[7] New Haven,[8] and elsewhere.[9] The housing transaction for Negro pioneers is very like that of their white neighbors. To be sure, the white realtor generally works to maintain segregated neighborhoods, but in this respect he is buttressed by traditions of prejudice and discrimination that are part of the entire social order. However, some realtors and many homeowners actively oppose these traditions in the public and the real estate industry.

HOW THE PROCESS OF PIONEERING OCCURS

This study essentially has been the account of how the process of pioneering occurred in fifteen neighborhoods of one northern city, with the stress placed on successful pioneering. How typical Seattle may be of other cities is unknown, and there are few similar studies of the subject elsewhere. Thus, a comparison is impossible.

Seattle's Negro population has doubled during the past decade. A major source of this growth has been through immigration. Colored migrants to the city for the most part have found dwellings in the Central Area, where most Negro families already lived.

In addition, they have expanded outward from the minority community, with fingers reaching in two directions—east to Lake Washington and south. The neighborhoods in our sample are located in all sectors of the city, never closer to its center than three miles.

Pioneer neighborhoods vary in many ways, but in almost every case they are single-family residential areas, where home ownership and median family income are higher than in the city as a whole.

The Negro and interracial families in our sample are well-educated, with stable, high incomes and a backlog of experience in interracial living. In these respects they are at a par or better than the typical resident of the neighborhood into which they move. Our pioneer families have not just arrived in the city, but have lived here for some time—usually in the minority community. For some of these families, this is not the first time they have pioneered in residential desegregation. They are resourceful people who have used all the usual sources of knowledge about the housing transaction, and then some in addition.

Almost without exception, the pioneer families do not see themselves as militant leaders in residential desegregation. They are people who can afford the homes they own. What they want in housing varies by the family, but in general a desire for more space, better schools, and a protected home investment led them to where they now live.

The difficulties invested in being the first Negro, or the only Negro family to live in a neighborhood, obviously play a part. Many of these first families availed themselves of the services of specialized social agencies (and white friends) to complete their purchases. Although the pioneer families are not "joiners" per se, the study shows that they are more likely to belong to neighborhood groups than their white neighbors. Even though they have moved out of the minority area, they continue to be active and influential as leaders in the Negro community.

The newcomers welcome visits from their neighbors and from local clubs, schools, and churches, as an indication of their acceptance in the neighborhood. Not all the pioneer families want to become active in local organizations. They are almost unanimous about wanting to be treated like others. They would rather not have visible social agency intervention in the integration process by the specialized human relations agencies, except perhaps in home-finding and the management of interracial crises.

The integration machinery varies from neighborhood to neighborhood. The fact that one fourth of our sample of white neighbors did not know that a Negro family lived within three blocks, is evidence that neighborhoods in general do not integrate all residents into one communications network. Some neighborhoods apparently were unconcerned with Negro entry.[10] They lacked formal or informal procedures for welcoming newcomers, Negro or white, and there was a relative dearth of local clubs and social life. These neighborhoods neither accepted nor rejected the Negro newcomers; they were not concerned.

On the other hand, some residents of other neighborhoods were strongly motivated to resist Negro entry and to oppose their attempts to become good neighbors. The roots of opposition are fed by many sources; there are many variations from neighborhood to neighborhood. Temporary residents of a neighborhood (such as students or renters) may express less concern than those whose residency is more permanent. There seemed to be less opposition among those who did not fear that the advent of a Negro family in their neighborhood was the forerunner of a mass influx. In some cases local realtors led the opposition—apparently because they feared a loss in property values.

Advance warning can take two forms: residents may be notified before the first Negro moves in, or white newcomers may be told that they will have a Negro neighbor already living there. Our study indicated that there was no single neighborhood reaction to advance warning of Negro entry: sometimes it seemed to engender more opposition; sometimes it seemed to pave the way; sometimes there was no apparent effect. In fact, antagonisms were more bitterly and more frequently expressed toward the seller of the housing than toward the Negro buyer.

The entry of the first Negro does not prevent further white settlement in the area. On the contrary, most recent white newcomers ignored the race of the next-door neighbor, and some welcomed this diversity.

In almost every case, the opposition to the Negro family has waned. The fears that most residents had about the entry failed to materialize. Sometimes the most vocal opponents moved away, but there was no mass exodus. In general, there were few changes in the neighborhood life; the Negro family fitted into the patterns much like any other newcomer. Few persons moved in or out of the neighborhood for racial reasons.

The pioneering process seems to have four stages: pre-entry, entry, accommodation, and integration. Neighborhoods do not inevitably pass through all stages in that order. Shared parental responsibility and concern often lead to early contacts. Most pioneer families felt that they were helped to become a part of the neighborhood after one of the older residents began to visit them and "broke the ice." Neighborhood children helped to bring about adult contacts, both because they found fewer barriers to social intercourse and because the schools and churches which they attended have traditional visitational practices. Parents met in the PTA's and churches and got to know each other there, and they carried their friendships back to the neighborhoods. In some places, the community club or "coffee klatch" was the center of organized opposition to Negro entry; there was less integration of the Negro families in these strictly social groups, as contrasted with the formal local institutions, the school and the church. Neighborliness apparently was not related to the educational level of the persons involved, nor to the nearness of their residence to the pioneer: next-door neighbors were not more friendly to the new Negro family than others who lived further away, nor were they less friendly.

Just as there was opposition to Negro entry, there was also support in the white community. Support came from both inside and outside the neighborhood into which the Negro families moved. Open housing lists, available through social agencies and membership organizations, provided housing for at least two of the pioneers. Once having moved in, Negroes in almost every neighborhood were visited by neighbors and local groups. Some neighbors arranged receptions and parties. Others gradually exchanged neighborly help. The reaching out by both the newcomer and the older resident seemed to be instrumental in getting settled. Social agencies, when they knew about the move, encouraged their members to extend a welcome to the newcomers. Where there were vandalism or threats of violence, the State Board Against Discrimination and others consulted the newcomer or, on a few occasions, visited neighbors. The attempts by prejudiced neighbors to buy out the newcomer received no encouragement from social agencies to whom they turned for help. Much of the work of the specialized community agencies was invisible to the residents of the neighborhoods. White neighbors were often opposed to such intervention. The Negro families did not feel that they received much help from the antidiscrimination network.

What can be done to improve pioneering as a strategy of desegregation? Some principles for effective service were suggested by this study and its aftermath. These are described according to the stages of the neighborhood integration process: pre-entry, entry, accommodation, and integration.

An "Open Housing" Listing Service
to Facilitate the Housing Transaction

Several informants spoke of the need for an effective open housing listing service. This would provide a direct route for buyers and sellers to avoid the detours of prejudice and discrimination during the housing transaction. The presence of a central listing service of open housing for minorities, of course, is prima-facie evidence that housing discrimination exists in a community, that this has been given public recognition, and that some steps are being taken to rectify the situation.

In the period, 1957-61, when the pioneer families reported in this study secured their homes, there was no effective open housing list in Seattle. To be sure, two of the families were helped by initial measures in this direction. For example, one pioneer family secured information about the house which they later purchased from an advertisement in the daily newspaper in which fourteen hundred persons pledged to receive bids from all races, when and if they contemplated selling or renting properties. This newspaper advertisement was the result of a campaign conducted by the Christian Friends for Racial Equality and other groups in 1959.[12] Similarly, a second family profited by the multiple-listing service of the Central Brokers Association.[13] This organization was established in 1960 by real estate brokers and investment brokers after the Seattle Real Estate Board had continually refused to make its lists available to Negroes. However, for the most part, the properties on the Central Brokers' list were located in the ghetto or at its borders.

In 1962, just after the completion of the interviewing for this study, two organizations—Harmony Homes, Inc., and the Fair Housing Listing Service—came into being, both of which have had marked success in helping Negro families to find housing out of the ghetto.[14] Though structurally independent of each other, the two groups share the same volunteer staff, plan activities conjointly, and work closely together with others in the antidiscrimination network. By July, 1964, the two groups were able to report that they had "directly negotiated fifty-two sales with a dollar volume over $1,000,000"—mostly for Negro families in predominantly white areas of Seattle and its suburbs. Moreover, through a listing of several hundred properties, Negro and white brokers were able to complete another estimated fifty sales on the open market. As a result, Harmony Homes stated in its *Newsletter*: [15]

> Too much success—we are working ourselves out of business. No new houses are in progress, as we are now able to refer buyers to hundreds of owners listing through the Fair Housing Listing Service.
> Our main function of opening up difficult areas through building is over, as we have made the initial start in dozens of places where other move-ins are now taking place. We are still going to use our funds to finance temporary mortgages. This is a service usually obtained quite easily by white buyers where brokers commonly aid them in transferring funds from the old house they sell to the new one.

Details on forty-two typical transactions were provided the authors by Sidney Gerber, the organizer of Harmony Homes and secretary of the Fair Housing Listing Service. Sixteen houses had been constructed by Harmony Homes during the two-year period, 1963-64, in nine middle-class neighborhoods, and three more in an area of Seattle occupied largely by Orientals. These were purchased by eighteen Negro families and one white family for prices ranging from $15,500 to $26,500. Usually the Negro family was the first or second to move into the neighborhood. Through the auspices of the Fair Housing Listing Service another twelve houses, ranging in price from $13,500 to $55,000, were sold to Negro families in white suburban areas. New buyers for Harmony Homes were located mostly by word of mouth from previous buyers, from notices in circulars and newsletters of cooperating organizations, handbills, and classified advertisements in the daily press. White and Negro real estate brokers were involved in six transactions. As the number of listings of the Fair Housing Listing Service increased, the tempo of housing construction diminished for Harmony Homes. During 1963-64, Harmony Homes purchased for Negroes two lots worth about $5,000 each on exclusive Mercer Island. Nine lots were also acquired in the Central Area for eight white families and one Negro family. This was part of a strategy to reinstate a favorable racial balance in this area.

The complementary functions of the two organizations are these: Where existing housing was not available for Negroes and other minorities, Harmony Homes acquired the land and built units itself. In this way, prospective Negro pioneers were able to take part in the selection of housing design and neighborhood rather than simply to purchase existing housing. In turn, unsold Harmony Homes were listed on the Fair Housing Listing Service together with others. The findings of this pioneer study are supported by the experiences of Harmony Homes and the Fair Housing Listing Service. They indicate certain principles of work that have been effective in overcoming racial discrimination during the housing transaction.

Broad range of services related to housing transaction. To be successful, the listing service should involve all the activities that are part of the housing transaction: the location of housing open to all buyers and renters regardless of race; help to the potential buyer in shopping for housing in a "strange, white neighborhood"; the availability of expert advice about housing values. Although a minority listing service may properly be considered an emergency program to be terminated after the establishment of an open housing market, the campaign to achieve this goal may be a long one. Besides the direct service to buyers and sellers, it may involve "tests" to secure the enforcement of existing laws and administrative rulings as well as following through to transform the successful tests into customary routines. In some cases, as in Seattle, a fund may be required to buy land, construct housing, and aid in its financing.

Stress on friendly neighborhood organization. Such a comprehensive program will require the cooperation of the antidiscrimination network, in particular locally based groups, such as churches and neighborhood clubs. In the minority community these will help to locate and encourage buyers to consider housing outside the ghetto. In white neighborhoods they can serve as a source of information about available housing, and act as welcoming committees for newcomers.

Organizational Autonomy. Although the listing service is dependent on the cooperation of the antidiscrimination network for maximum utility, it may wish to maintain independent organizational status with single focus on problems in the housing transaction. Such autonomy provides freedom to initiate actions necessary to secure this house for this person, now. Harmony Homes, for example, as an autonomous limited-profit corporation responsible only to its ten shareholders, can assume financial risks that are ruled out for most social agencies. In a similar way, the Fair Housing Listing Service is sponsored by eighteen church organizations—Catholic, Protestant, and Jewish—plus CORE, NAACP, the Anti-Defamation League, the Urban League, and Harmony Homes, Inc.; nevertheless, it maintains the autonomy necessary to accomplish its stated goals.

Nonprofit Status. One requirement for a successful listing service apparently is its nonprofit status. The users of the Fair Housing Listing Service have not been charged a fee; Harmony Homes has restricted dividends to its stockholders to 6 per cent per annum. There are no paid staff members of the organizations. The small budget of about $300 per year required by the Listing Service comes from good-will contributions. As a consequence, the two groups have been able to secure broad organizational support and the voluntary services of professional and technical persons with knowledge of the law and housing. As the services of such agencies become more demanding in time and skills of the volunteer staff, a budget for salaried staff and overhead may become necessary.

Customarily, the housing transaction is business which flows through the hands of the real estate agency. Human relations and social welfare agencies have scrupulously avoided competition with realtors, but instead have sought to utilize their expertness.

When most large realtors refuse to observe open housing practices, however, the listing service must assume that responsibility. Thus, every housing transaction completed by the listing service reduces the market for private enterprise.

Furthermore, the ethics that govern the conduct of the listing service sometimes are at variance with those of the industry. The listing service is usually required to exclude houses that are outrageously overpriced and also those that come on the market because of neighborhood conflict. In order to maintain the confidence of the Negro buyer, who is frequently exploited in his housing transactions, and also to uphold the reputation of its sponsors, the listing service emphasizes protection for the consumer rather than efforts to maximize the profit or a policy of "Let the buyer beware!"

Relationships between realtors and a listing service become especially strained in the practice of blockbusting. Blockbusters use the fears and prejudices of whites to get them to sell their property below its value after the advent of the first Negro resident.[16] Such property is quickly resold only to Negro purchasers until the neighborhood has completely changed its racial composition. Blockbusting as a tactic has been used to secure scarce housing for Negroes. But the practice reinforces the prejudices that lead to racial segregation. The tactic of pioneering is also dedicated to securing scarce housing for Negroes; but, in principle, it is in direct opposition to blockbusting, for pioneering is aimed at promoting racial accommodation and integration rather than prejudice and segregation.

The listing service is an enemy of the realtor-blockbuster. Indeed, one of the major goals of the listing service is to assure stability in the racial composition of neighborhoods.

Harmony Homes and the Fair Housing Listing Service both employ some informal racial quotas.[17] In building new houses next to each other, these organizations make an all-out effort to secure buyers of different races. Older houses are purchased where there is only one vacant unit for sale on the block, and special measures are taken with neighbors to promote good feelings for the Negro newcomer. When new listings are sought in an active organizational campaign, the emphasis is placed on locating neighborhoods with no minority residents. Through the use of such informal quota practices, it may be possible to avoid drastic changes in neighborhood racial composition.

Such quota practices, at best, are difficult to enforce and are the subject of much controversy among civil rights proponents. The authors know of no instance in Seattle in which "invasion" or "flooding" has occurred in the wake of a first Negro resident. However, location of the neighborhoods involved and the relatively high cost of the houses chosen may have been important deterrents to the development of such a situation.

Prejudice, racial segregation, and lack of concern cause many problems for the listing service, especially during the period of shopping for housing. Peoples who are kept separate by custom or coercion remain strangers. Consequently, many Negroes are reluctant to live among whites. They, too, are subject to many doubts and fears concerning such integration. Like whites, they hope to find a friendly neighborhood in which to purchase a home. The first visit, whether driving through a neighborhood or visiting a house listed for sale, is a critical time for assessing the friendliness of the neighborhood. For this reason, special attempts are made by the Listing Service to accompany prospective Negro buyers while they are shopping for homes and to arrange for their friendly reception while inspecting houses for sale or rent.

Measures to familiarize prospective Negro buyers with housing in predominantly white neighborhoods can be taken on an individual or on a mass basis. The Listing Service acts primarily on a case-by-case basis. In the summer of 1963, however, the Seattle CORE organized a series of weekend "Operation Windowshops." The intention was to have Negro couples—sometimes in the company of a white friend—visit tract homes, which realtors had advertised as open to the public. The program was announced in the daily newspapers.

On the first weekend of "Operation Windowshop," 95 per cent of the real estate offices were reported to be closed, according to the Seattle *Times* of July 31, 1963. The executive vice-president of the Seattle Real Estate Board reportedly said that "the realtors who closed apparently wanted time to consult with their attorneys and figure out how the action could be reasonably met." [18] He also stated that there was no organized movement among realtors to close their doors to Negro shoppers. He charged that civil rights advocates had designed a parade of Negroes, who had no intention of buying homes, through houses on sale in areas outside the Central Area. In reply, the secretary of the Fair Housing Listing Service told of his efforts during the weekend to help a Negro couple find a home in the $20,000 to $25,000 range, concentrating in the Newport Hills area east of Lake Washington.[19]

> The real-estate offices were all closed and there were no open-house signs in an area that the prior week had been covered with signs. A white man and woman trailed us all the way in another car, making caustic remarks.

On the other hand, some neighborhood churches and sympathetic persons living in the areas being visited arranged teas and receptions for the shoppers.

Despite differences with realtors and others in the housing industry, listing services have had accomplishments as well as setbacks, as indicated by two further experiences of Harmony Homes: [20]

> Lochmoor—a typical medium to high priced tract of new homes with entrance gate, overlooking Lake Sammamish, is controlled by one of the largest builders and a prominent realtor. Charges against them have been made for years with the State Board Against Discrimination and the FHA, but they still maintained their exclusive policy, like all the other subdivisions using FHA services. Recently we met with many organizations forming the Fair Housing Listing Service, who protested in letters and wires to Washington, D.C., that the Executive Order on housing was being ignored here. After this pressure we secured the co-operation of the acting director of FHA in Seattle and negotiated a signed contract directly between the builder and the first Negro purchaser.
>
> This was the first known transaction between a large tract builder in a good residential area of Seattle involving a sale of a new home to a Negro, even though the bulk of such financing has involved FHA, and brokers have been classified as a place of public accommodation. It is the real start. The builder will now cooperate on all his tracts, and currently several families are inspecting his houses in another 100% pure division. The now Regional Director of FHA has met with us and assured his interest in our program. We take the position that any builder using substantial FHA services must serve equally in *all* his houses, not just offering several of his least desirable ones to minorities. We have a volunteer committee to ac-

company buyers to sub-divisions, compare prices, and explain use of the law.

Postscript: No, not again? When we sold the first home (in Newport Hills) last year ever purchased by a Negro, we thought the ruling realtors there might mellow, but it is still being done the hard way. Two more Negro families are in the process of buying, both through Fair Housing Listing Service, and Harmony Homes has again had to step in and aid one of the deals with some interim financing.

The first steps toward the establishment of a minority listing service have been taken in Seattle. The success of this service apparently is the result of a combination of factors: skillful, dedicated volunteers; a housing market characterized by high vacancy rates; and full support from the entire antidiscrimination network. The results of the case studies of pioneering prior to 1962 are borne out in the experiences of dozens of other families after that time. The advance warning of a public listing apparently does *not* deter entry of the first Negro family. There have been relatively few examples of malicious spite and none of violence in the cases reported. There has been *no* Negro invasion and *no* white mass exodus. However, barriers of pluralistic ignorance and prejudice still remain and slow down desegregation. Although an increasing number of small Negro and white real estate offices have joined the listing service, large realtors remain skeptical and reluctant to cooperate.

The Seattle CORE has also conducted other types of activities to facilitate housing transactions for Negroes. It has organized "sit-ins" in the offices of large white realty concerns which have refused to conduct business with Negroes on the same terms as whites. It has encouraged prospective Negro buyers to attend builders' shows and to take part in events which visibly demonstrate their interest in open housing. In 1964 plans are under way to secure the employment of qualified Negro brokers in large white real estate businesses which hire as many as fifty employees. CORE alleges that refusal to employ qualified Negroes is liable to prosecution under the State Fair Employment Practices Act and also may be covered by administrative rulings that apply to federally financed housing.

THE FAIR HOUSING LAW AS AN AID TO THE HOUSING TRANSACTION

An open housing listing service brings on the market properties that the owners and their representatives voluntarily wish to see available to all qualified buyers regardless of race, color, or creed. It does not bring on the market properties that the owners do not wish to see listed in this way. Listing services, experience shows, account for only a tiny fraction of the needed housing. Although open listing is a valuable service, it is not sufficient to assure an open housing market. Another measure to facilitate such a goal is fair housing legislation.[21]

Currently, many restrictions are placed on private housing with respect to building and safety standards, and neighborhoods are zoned for compatible uses and to protect property values. Fair housing legislation would merely extend these practices to bring the private housing sector into line with principles of constitutional law and democracy.

The extension of democracy to the private housing market has continually run into challenges that it improperly restricts individual rights and the conduct of private business. Fortunately, there has been sufficient experience with such legislation as it exists in twelve states and other jurisdictions to compile much factual information on the subject. A recent review clearly shows that such legislation has not resulted in the dire consequences predicted. Several hundred complaints have been made under these laws, almost all of which were settled out of court without need for imposition of fines or jail sentences, and to the satisfaction of the complainants.[22]

The presence of a fair housing law in the state of Washington provided the sanction for workers of the State Board Against Discrimination to intervene on behalf of five pioneer families in our sample when they requested help. It was not necessary to go to court with respect to any of these cases. Somewhat later, however, the Washington law was challenged in court, and some sections were voided as being in violation of the state Constitution.[23] Concerted efforts in 1963-64 to secure adequate legislation of this sort from the Washington State Legislature and the city of Seattle failed to pass. During this period Superior Court Judge Eugene

Wright ruled that the old Washington Public Accommodation Law covers brokers, and this ruling has not yet been upset in any higher court.

Pioneering and legislative enactment should be seen as mutually reinforcing courses of action. Open housing legislation is needed to make it possible to penalize overt acts of discrimination and to set a tone of public morality compatible with democracy. Pioneering is required to test the effectiveness of the enforcement of the law, to point to the gaps in public morality, as an educational device for the general public, and as an effective method of finding housing for minorities. Relocation programs in urban renewal cannot hope to comply with their own legal and administrative requirements for nondiscrimination and adequate rehousing of minorities unless there is incorporated into their administration an effective service for pioneers.

HELP AT TIME OF ENTRY

Pioneering in Seattle has been accomplished with little violence or serious vandalism, apparently because threats to law and order were met firmly by the city police, the City Planning Department in the one instance where it was consulted, and the State Board Against Discrimination. Informants were unanimously in support of firm control over violence and vandalism, and this was the only kind of help about which there was unanimity.

It is a short step from laws for maintaining the peace and preventing property damage to laws designed to curtail discrimination in the housing transaction, as we have shown in the last section. The major impact of such laws is that they create and shape public morality, which is invaluable in helping to overcome problems of entry and establishment of the Negro newcomer in a white neighborhood.

A law cannot guarantee a friendly welcome. This is a more personal matter. In the era of the "organization man," the average citizen often feels that there is almost nothing he can do by himself to combat racial discrimination. However, the person with a home for sale can entertain bids from all qualified persons without respect to their race, creed, or ethnic origin. Another direct action is to be neighborly toward any minority newcomer.

Our study underlined the significance of friendly visiting by neighbors and by the representatives of neighborhood churches and schools. Not only were these visits welcomed by the Negro newcomers; such visits also seemed to be directly associated with the tempo of neighborhood acceptance of the newcomers. Moreover, calls by the specialized city agencies do not substitute for local friendly visiting.

SPECIALIZED HUMAN RELATIONS AGENCIES AND CREATION OF A TOLERANT CLIMATE OF OPINION

How can Seattle create and nurture a climate of opinion that will help to bring about tolerance and permit an open housing market to exist with a minimum of friction? What can social agencies and citizen groups do to foster such a condition?

The preceding sections have discussed activities that depended for their effectiveness on the fact that they were direct, visible, and evident. There can be no equivocation in police enforcement of law and order in neighborhoods. In addition, the law must be sufficient to curtail unfair business practices and to assure equal opportunity. To do this, its provisions must be known and applied. A listing service is open to the public, and its use should be encouraged. Even the private act of a friendly visit, when noted, serves to inform the neighborhood publicly that the newcomer is welcomed.

Many programs, activities, and services are not directly related to facilitating the housing transaction or neighborhood accommodation. For example, various agencies continually conduct broad educational programs on issues of prejudice and discrimination. Educational activities in Seattle have great scope (as noted in table 3, page 61), but it is difficult to assess their full contribution to the democratic climate of opinion. Social research methods are gradually being developed for such evaluation. The findings of research filter back through the specialized intergroup agencies to professional practice.

The specialized intergroup agencies are in a difficult position. They are continually being challenged to do more to end prejudice and discrimination. The nature of their work must be sufficiently visible and direct so that they will continue to receive

public support, whether in the form of tax dollars, private dona-
tions, or memberships. At the same time, to be effective, much of
their work must be unobtrusive, or preferably invisible, according
to many of our respondents. The executives of many agencies
have found that it is difficult to take direct action on issues as
value-laden as racial and religious prejudices and still maintain
year-round working relationships. For example, a city human
rights commission might be reluctant to criticize the discriminatory hiring practices of another city agency, or to take public issue
with the mayor on civil rights. Similar "gentlemen's agreements"
may exist among private social agencies—"We will not criticize
you if you do not criticize us."

We have already commented on the myths and half-truths with
respect to interracial living that permeate both the popular cul-
ture and the business and professional communities. This mythology gradually is being identified. Nevertheless, the proper courses
of action for better education of public opinion remain uncertain.
For example, this small study has indicated that there is no one
neighborhood reaction to advance warning of Negro entry. Also,
this report cannot indicate with certainty when, and under what
conditions, a pre-entry educational campaign would be successful.
One cannot know how such a campaign should be conducted to
have the best results. Thus to mythology is added ambiguity.
Some myths have been weakened, but they have not been replaced
with certain answers.

In the final analysis, the process of pioneering deals with the
housing problem of a particular set of people. It is largely a phenomenon of the *private housing market*. When housing is part of
the *public* sector, and dwelling units are assigned rather than
selected by their occupant, there are quite different problems of
prejudice, discrimination, and segregation; and they can be dealt
with differently. The fact that pioneering deals with the private
housing market is an added complication in working out feasible
solutions.

Usually there has been a sufficient harmony of interests between
social agencies and citizen groups to establish a workable *modus
operandi* when the target was the general reduction of prejudice
and discrimination. The antidiscrimination agencies have been
able to function reasonably well on moral problems and to estab-

lish ameliorative educational programs. As emphasis is placed more directly on housing and neighborhood desegregation and this activity moves into the private housing sector, greater stresses and strains may be expected among the principal groups concerned with the housing problem. This conflict is clearly apparent in the unwillingness of the real estate industry to accept open housing ordinances. In Seattle, and elsewhere, however, there are schisms within the real estate business on this issue.

THE POTENTIALS OF PIONEERING FOR DESEGREGATION

Assuming that all the housing problems of pioneer families can be worked out, will this solve the *minority* housing problem? Obviously the answer is "No." However, the potential of the pioneering strategy should be one basis for structuring the services of agencies in the antidiscrimination network.

The paragraphs that follow contain a brief analysis of the nonwhite housing market in Seattle. [24] We will attempt to determine the relative buying power of the nonwhite minorities as contrasted with the white majority. Then by comparison with similar statistics estimated for the pioneers in our sample, it will be possible to secure an answer to the question: at what economic level should pioneering take place in order to open the housing market to the average Negro wage earner?

Table 4 presents a comparison of the statements of white and nonwhite families in Seattle as to the gross rent or the housing value of the dwelling unit in which they resided at the time of the 1960 census. These estimates can be taken as a modest estimate of what the residents could afford to pay for housing at that time. It is apparent that nonwhites live in housing with lesser estimated value than whites. For example, 10 per cent of the nonwhites lived in housing valued at $15,000 or more as contrasted with 24 per cent of the whites. However, approximately six of every ten families, both white and nonwhite, live in housing valued between $5,000 and $15,000 or pay rents of over $60 per month.

In contrast to the general estimate above is the estimated value of the housing of the twenty-one pioneer families for which we have such information. The median value of their homes is $17,-

TABLE 4

COMPARISON OF WHITE AND NONWHITE FAMILIES IN VALUE OF PROPERTY
AND GROSS MONTHLY RENTAL IN SEATTLE, 1960 *

Value of Property	or Gross Rent per Month	Number of Families		Per Cent of Families	
		White	Nonwhite	White	Nonwhite
Totals		180,534	13,854	100	102
$25,000 or more		10,054	114	6	1
$24,900-$20,000		8,200	208	5	2
$19,900-$15,000		22,170	854	13	8
$14,900-$10,000	or $100 and over	59,306	3,121	32	23
$ 9,900-$ 5,000	or $ 99-$60	54,346	4,996	30	36
$ 4,900-X	or $ 59-$40	14,951	2,151	8	15
	$ 39-$20	8,581	1,843	5	13
	$ 19-X	424	141	. .	1
	No cash rent	2,502	426	1	3

* Sources: U.S. Bureau of Census, *U.S. Censuses of Population and Housing: 1960, Census Tracts, Seattle, Washington,* Final Report PHC(1)–142, pp. 129, 177.

000. Three quarters of the sample of pioneer families owned homes valued in excess of $15,000; about one third of the houses were worth $30,000 or more. It has been shown that these Negro pioneers have relatively high stable incomes and are able to afford the housing of their choice—housing that is beyond the economic level of 90 per cent of the nonwhite families in Seattle.

Apparently, pioneering was a successful strategy for solving the housing problems of Negro families with sufficient, stable incomes, who were resourceful and experienced in problems of interracial living. To be within the reach of the large majority of Negro families, however, pioneering will need to take place in neighborhoods containing housing within the $5,000 to $15,000 price range. As yet, not many houses of this sort in Seattle are coming on the market through voluntary listing. A concerted campaign in medium-priced housing may increase the number of neighborhoods where pioneering is an effective strategy. There is still much room in Seattle and elsewhere for such efforts, but in the long run, "trickle down" theories have *not* produced large quantities of housing for middle- and lower-income families, and it seems unlikely that pioneering will be the major strategy for solving the minority housing problem.[25]

Pioneering as an Antidote to Pluralistic Ignorance

The main value of the pioneering strategy, in the long run, may be the evidence it provides of the feasibility of interracial neighboring. The willingness of white Americans to tolerate practices of discrimination, even though they may deny any racial prejudice in themselves, has been seen as one of the most stubborn barriers to neighborhood integration. For example, people will not place their homes on the open market in deference to "what neighbors may think."

Public opinion studies in Seattle and across the nation have shown drastic changes in attitudes toward having a Negro neighbor. In 1926, one study found 90 per cent of the respondents unwilling to live in integrated neighborhoods.[26] In 1948, only 60 per cent of the national sample replied in this way.[27] In 1956, the proportion of persons who would not like to have a Negro neighbor was reduced to about 50 per cent; this study found younger people more in favor of integration than the general average.[28]

Similar findings were reported for Seattle and the Northwest. In 1949, a Seattle Health and Welfare Council Study noted that 69 per cent of the white respondents would not like Negroes "as next-door neighbors," but 53 per cent said, "if a Negro family moved next door . . . they would accept them like any other neighbor," or would "go out of [their] way to make them feel wanted." [29] In the period from 1954 to 1956, Portland studies found that proximity to Negroes correlated highly with attitudes supporting integration.[30] Significantly, many persons who supported segregation believed that their neighbors also favored segregation, but few who supported integration felt that their neighbors agreed with them.

The findings of this study clearly buttress the earlier ones in the following two ways. Earlier in the book it was noted that only about 10 per cent of the white families who knew of the presence of Negro neighbors were "unhappy" or "very unhappy" about this; about 40 per cent (twenty-three families) said they were "very happy" or "happy"; and the balance were "neutral" on the subject. Thus, from the facts and opinions collected, it appears that residential desegregation can take place in a reasonably harmonious manner. The data in these cases are limited to neighborhoods in which pioneering has occurred; therefore, no generalizations can be made that apply to all sections of Seattle. However, the pioneer neighborhoods were much more favorable to desegregation than the reaction indicated by a poll of Seattle residents taken a decade earlier by the Seattle Health and Welfare Council. This trend throughout the city is consistent with changing attitudes elsewhere in the nation.

The second way in which this study supports the earlier work is that, once again, it provides evidence of pluralistic ignorance. The respondents to our study did not believe that their neighbors were as favorable to the pioneer family as the survey actually demonstrated. This pluralistic ignorance was found in one third of our respondents. They were inaccurate in their estimates of the reactions of the people who lived nearby about an event that the neighborhood had actually experienced.

Pluralistic ignorance emerges when there is a lack of communication or when social attitudes on the issue have been undergoing rapid change. Neighborhoods usually are not cohesive, interacting social groups except for those subsections consisting of neighbors living next to one another. Certainly, little communication exists in an area if the news of a Negro family in the neighborhood has not traveled a block or two after they have resided there for years.

Americans are suffering from a legacy that stresses social distance and hostility between Negroes and whites. This legacy is reinforced through segregation and buttressed by daily accounts of racial antagonism. Discrimination is rationalized as something fixed because "people are prejudiced," which is a frequent excuse for failure to act for such goals as open housing. The realtor suffers from pluralistic ignorance when he refuses to show homes in white areas to Negroes because he believes they will not be acceptable to whites as neighbors. In turn, his acts often serve to perpetuate this myth.

The pluralistic ignorance of a large proportion of the white neighbors in this study did not prevent their acceptance of the Negro newcomer; nevertheless, it may impede further desegregation. On the other hand, the ignorance of many realtors can be instrumental in denying to such neighborhoods changes that are imminent and long overdue.

So far pluralistic ignorance has been seen as a brake to social change, but it may also act in a contrary manner, as in the practice of blockbusting. In blockbusting, realtors use the fears and prejudices of whites to convince them to sell their property cheaply after the advent of the first Negro resident.[31] The realtor quickly resells this property to Negro purchasers only, until the neighborhood has completely changed its racial composition. In this way, pluralistic ignorance facilitates a drastic turnover, but the principles of segregation remain unchanged—the ghetto is merely extended. Although some attempts were made, blockbusting did not succeed in the sections of Seattle studied in this book. Blockbusting seems to occur in areas adjacent to the Negro ghetto, and none of the sample areas were located there.

No single program by itself is likely to solve the minority housing problem. Pioneering is one effective strategy for starting the desegregation process. An open listing aids the housing transaction. Enforcement of the law, including a fair housing law, will help to curtail violations of person and property, reduce unfair business practices, clarify public morality, and stimulate the minority search for housing. Programs of education and research by specialized human relations agencies are needed to promote neighborhood accommodation and integration. There is no substitute for direct action by each citizen to encourage tolerance and neighborliness. All of these measures, in concert, help desegregation.

The advent of the first Negro family alters the segregated fabric of an all-white neighborhood, but it will not assure continuation of the desegregation process until open housing conditions pertain throughout the city. Nor does the solution of the housing problems of relatively affluent pioneer families deal directly with the housing problems of middle- and lower-income classes—Negro or white. To solve the minority housing problem requires a coordinated approach by housing, human relations, and social services agencies, which traditionally have worked piecemeal and separately.[32] Urban renewal programs are bringing the three together, but many barriers still remain before adequate housing is provided for all Americans.

An Agenda of Research

This study was based on cases of successful pioneering in one city. It should be repeated elsewhere. Our characterization of the neighborhood is based on interviews with six persons, and a larger number of respondents would probably be preferable. The researchers should also assess neighborhoods that fail, as well as those in which there is success.

The findings suggest that not all neighborhoods within a metropolitan community are similar in their reactions to social change. Neighborhoods were selected on the basis of the presence of a first Negro family. Future researchers may want to select neighborhoods according to other criteria as well, such as family composition, income class of residents, distance from city center, prior change of racial composition, and so forth. For example, neighborhoods might be rated on a tolerance-intolerance dimension, as well as on the basis of the residents' assessment of the likelihood of change in the neighborhood's racial composition. Such a fourfold typology undoubtedly would have significance for the planning of controlled neighborhood desegregation.

We have proposed a four-stage theory of the neighborhood integration process. Although the observations recorded in this research are in accord with this theory, a great deal remains to be explained. What factors hasten or hinder the process? Respondents' opinions on this question were solicited, but the survey data should be supplemented with many more periodic observations of families undergoing the same process. Attention should be given to detailed examination of the activities of all members of the Negro family and their white neighbors, local neighborhood clubs and institutions, and the specialized city-wide agencies.

What pays off in smoother and more effective integration? Is it education of children by their parents on how to conduct themselves to promote racial amity? Is it the adoption of a conciliatory or firm stance by the pioneer family to unfriendly acts by their neighbors? Is it direct intervention of local neighborhood clubs to help in the desegregation process? At the present time, we cannot state with certainty what particular course of action will inevitably have the best or worst results, or even specify the conditions under which to work most effectively. This book includes many anecdotes, and also some systematic information on the subject, which could be translated into more fruitful research.

We have suggested that in many localities the neighborhood is not an interacting social group, except for small clusters of persons living next-door to one another. Some of the findings suggest that the residents' attitudes about good neighbors and neighboring appear to be influenced more by tradition than by actual experiences with their neighbors. This frequently results in a kind of pluralistic ignorance, which under some conditions tends to minimize socially undesirable conflict; in other cases it is an impediment to residential desegregation. Research about pluralistic ignorance is necessary if its negative consequences are to be controlled.

The relevance of the neighborhood to urban life has been bypassed frequently in favor of large-scale studies of urban land use, population movements, and institutional development. In order fully to understand these bigger problems, it is necessary also to examine the inner dynamics of the neighborhood integration process. The findings of research, implemented with direct action, can bring us closer to the realization of equal opportuntiy in housing for all.

Appendix A

PIONEER FAMILY: FIRST INTERVIEW

(Introduction) "Good evening. I'm _____ (and this is _____). We are from the University of Washington on the neighborhood relations project that Dr. _____ called you about. We appreciate the opportunity you've given to us to ask you some questions. We want to say again that any information you give us is completely confidential."

1. First of all, when did you first move into this neighborhood? Then you've lived here since _____?
2. Where did you live before moving in this home?
3. As a child what state did you grow up in?
   a. Is that where you lived most of your life?
   b. (If no, ask) Where did you live mostly, then?
   c. How about your wife (husband)? Where did she live mostly?
4. Are you buying or do you rent this house?
5. What factors helped you to decide on moving to this neighborhood?
6. When you first moved here, did any of the neighbors call to welcome you to the neighborhood? (If yes, ask) Would you tell me about that?
7. When you first moved into this neighborhood, did any organized groups officially send visitors or come to see you?
   a. (If yes, ask) Would you tell me about that?
   b. (If no, ask) And since then have you had any such visits?
   c. How do you feel about this?
8. "Now, I would like to ask you a few questions about your

children." First, how many children under 21 do you have living with you here? Name and age of each.

9. Do any of your children (under 21 and over 5 only) belong to organizations or clubs which are located in this neighborhood?
   a. (If no, ask) Can you tell me why they haven't joined any neighborhood clubs?
   b. (If yes, ask) How about your oldest child (under 21)? What neighborhood groups does he belong to?
   c. (For each organization mentioned, ask) How did he (she) happen to join that organization?
   d. What about your second oldest child? What neighborhood groups does he (she) belong to? How did he (she) happen to join.
   e. What about your third oldest child? What neighborhood groups does he (she) belong to? How did he (she) join?

10. Do your children belong to any organizations and clubs which are not located in this neighborhood?
    (If yes, ask) What organizations are these?

11. Are there children in the neighborhood whose ages are about the same as your children's?
    a. (If yes, ask) How often do your children and the other children of this neighborhood play together?
    b. Have your children ever experienced any hostility from the children here in the neighborhood or at school?
       (If yes, ask) Would you care to tell of these experiences?

12. How do you think your children get along with the adults in the neighborhood?

13. "Now let's switch to some different questions." Was there any opposition to your moving to this neighborhood when you first moved here? (If no, go to question 14)
    (If yes, ask) Would you care to describe this? (Probe)
    a. Has this opposition persisted to the present?
    b. How do you account for its ceasing?

14. Is this the kind of neighborhood in which neighbors visit each other frequently?

15. Do you visit your neighbors in their homes?
    (If yes, ask) How frequently do you make these visits to each other?

16. Do your Caucasian neighbors visit you in your home?
    (If yes, ask) How often do these neighbors come to visit you?
17. After living here for awhile, do you think there has been any change in the general attitude of your neighbors toward you since you first moved into this neighborhood?
    (If yes, ask) How do you think these attitudes have changed?
    (If yes, ask) What, in your opinion, do you think is the cause of this change in attitude?
18. Have you ever experienced any hostility from any of your neighbors or shopkeepers in this area?
    (If yes, ask) Would you care to describe these incidents?
19. Now, I'm wondering about the groups you belong to. First, do you belong to any clubs or organizations located in *this* neighborhood? (If no, skip to question 20)
    (If yes, ask) What organizations are these? (For each organization mentioned, ask) How did you happen to join? (Enter responses in box. Indicate with "H," "W" or "B" [both] who belong)
20. (If no to 19, ask) Is there any special reason why you haven't joined any local neighborhood groups?
    (Probe) Have you or your wife ever been invited to join any local groups?
21. Do you feel that you would be welcomed by others in the group if you were to join a local group?
    Why is that?
22. Do you attend a church located in this neighborhood?
    a. (If yes, ask) Are you a member of this church?
    b. How did you happen to start with this church?

"Now let's turn to a different topic: I have a list of community agencies which are located in Seattle." (Hand list to respondent)

23. In your search for housing and in establishing yourself here in this neighborhood, did you have any contact with one or another of these agencies?
    (If no, skip to question 26)
    (If yes, ask) What agencies are these? (For each agency identified, ask) How was that agency involved? What did they do?

LIST OF AGENCIES

—Home Builder's Association of Greater Seattle
—Labor union organizations
—Local Citizen's Council
—Local church
—Local police
—State Board Against Discrimination
—Local Public Schools
—PTA
—Real Estate Board
—Civic Unity Committee
—Urban League
—Businessmen's Clubs: such as Chamber of Commerce, Merchants' Association, Rotary
—Local Service Organizations: such as Eagles, Eastern Star, Elks, Kiwanis, Lions, Masons
—Seattle Housing Authority
—Christian Friends for Racial Equality
—United Good Neighbors
—Youth Groups: such as Boy, Girl Scouts
—NAACP
—Anti-Defamation League of B'nai B'rith

24. Were there any *other* agencies you had contact with that are *not* on this list?
    (If yes, ask) What agencies were these? What did they do?
25. (If respondent had contact with agencies, ask) Do you feel that what the agencies did was helpful or not helpful?
    Why do you feel that way?
26. In moving in and establishing yourself in the neighborhood did you ask for help from any community agencies and not receive it?
    Would you mind telling me about that?
27. How do you think agency services in this regard could be improved?
28. What do you feel agencies can do or should do that would have been helpful to you and others having the same experience?

"Now we have a different set of questions."

29. How do you think your presence in this neighborhood has or will affect the value of the property in this area?

30. Have you made any improvements in your property since you moved into the neighborhood?
    (If yes, ask) What type of improvements have you made?

31. Are you buying or do you rent this house?

32. (If buying, ask) How much is the approximate value of the house?
    (If renting, ask) How much is your monthly rent?

33. How did you originally learn about this house being available?

34. Would you care to comment on how you secured the house?

35. Would you describe any difficulties you encountered in financing the house? (Probe) How did you overcome these difficulties?

36. Could you pass along any general information about your experiences in moving and getting established here that might be useful to others who might be anticipating similar experiences?

37. What is your occupation? Does your wife work? What does she do?

38. What are your ages? Husband's _____ Wife's _____

39. (Hand respondent income category card and say) Here's a card showing categories of income. In what category does your family belong?

a.__Under $2000 annually	f.__$6000 – 6999
b.__$2000 – 2999	g.__$7000 – 7999
c.__$3000 – 3999	h.__$8000 – 8999
d.__$4000 – 4999	i.__$9000 – 9999
e.__$5000 – 5999	j.__$10,000 – 14,000
	k.__Over $14,000

40. What is the last school year you completed?
    And your wife? (Husband)

"And now, thank you for your help in this study."

PIONEER FAMILY: SECOND INTERVIEW

As you know, we have interviewed approximately twenty-five persons who are like yourself—one of the first minority residents in a predominantly white area. Our analysis of our first interviews is providing us with much valuable information about how segregation and desegregation occur. However, there are certain gaps in our information, and that is why we are taking this second interview.

In particular we would like to ask you some questions that will allow us to see how segregation and integration have been woven into your life. This makes it necessary for me to ask you some questions about the neighborhood you grew up in and to get some further information about your life in Seattle now.

1. First, let's start with the neighborhood you lived in as a child. From our earlier interview I notice that was in the state of: Husband _____ Wife _____.

2. Will you tell me what city or town you lived in as a child: Husband _____ Wife _____.

3. Can you tell me—was the immediate neighborhood you lived in as a child a segregated neighborhood? By neighborhood, we mean the block you lived on and the area right around it.

   I have a card here. (Give card. Enter answer in table) Can you tell me which of these categories best describes the neighborhood you lived in as a child? (read categories) (1) all Negro, (2) mostly Negro, (3) about 50-50, (4) mostly white, (5) all white except for one or two Negro families. (Repeat question for grade school, junior high, high school, church.)

4. College (for those attending): Was the college you attended all Negro __, integrated __, or other __.
   What city was that college located in?

5. Now let's turn back to the church your family attended when you were a child. Which one of the categories on the card best describes the membership of the church your family attended?

6. (If answered) What specific denomination was that church?

7. Which of the categories on the card best describes your church?

8. Now I'd like to ask you a few more questions about the nature of segregation as you have experienced it during your life-

time. Going back to your childhood, was the segregation you ran into legally required or would you say it just grew up as a natural thing?

9. How about your family, did they have any white friends?

(If yes,) Looking at the card I gave you, which of those categories best describes the friends of your family?

10. What race were your parents? (Husband and wife)

11. Now about yourself.

Would you say that over your lifetime you have ever had a really close friend who was white?

How did that come about?

12. Now I'd like you to think about your three best friends right here in Seattle—the people you feel closest to. Where does your first friend live? The second? The third?

13. Do you have any relatives here in the Seattle area?

What relationship are they and where do they live?

14. Now coming back to your first friend (second friend, etc.), is he Negro or Caucasian?

15. About how often do you see these friends in an average month?

(1) Daily, (2) Once a week or more, (3) Once a month or more, (4) Less than once a month.

16. Now about the organizations you belong to.

During the past three years, have you (or your spouse) ever been an officer of any organization or association? (Details)

17. Now let's shift to another area of questions.

Moving into a different neighborhood always means some change in accustomed ways. What differences would you say your present move has made to your family?

18. Are there things you miss as a result of moving into a predominantly white neighborhood?

19. What things do you really miss by not living in a Negro neighborhood?

20. To what extent would you say this is true of all Negroes moving into predominantly white neighborhoods?

21. Do you think that light skin color has any effect on the success or failure of Negroes to find housing in a predominantly white area?

(If it isn't skin color, then what?)

22. If no, do you think that light skin color has any effect on the success or failure of Negroes to get along once they have moved in?

23. Do you think in your own case that skin color of yourself or your wife had any effect on your success in moving in here?

24. Can you recall *any* experience that occurred to you where skin color rather than race as such made a difference? If yes, why do you say that?

25. Would you say that in your case you have had reason to acquire different attitudes toward integration since you moved into this neighborhood? (Why do you say that?)

26. How does your wife (husband) feel about this in contrast to you? (Since husband and wife often have different attitudes about some or many things.)

27. You were asked at the end of the first interview whether you had any general information to pass along for the benefit of others who might be contemplating a similar move. Is there anything you wish to add at this time?

28. Do you feel that our interviews in the neighborhood have had any effects on the attitudes of neighbors or anything else?
   (If yes,) In what way?

29. Would you be interested in receiving a copy of the final report when it is ready?

WHITE NEIGHBOR INTERVIEW

(Introduction) "Good evening. The Neighborhood Research Project of the University of Washington is presently engaged in a large scale study of neighborhood relations. We are calling on a cross-section of persons living in this neighborhood and would greatly appreciate an opportunity to ask you a few questions. We want you to know that any information you give us is completely confidential."

1. First of all, when did you first move into this neighborhood? Then you've lived here since _____?

2. Where did you live before moving to this home?

3. As a child, what state did you grow up in?

    a. Is that where you lived most of your life?

    b. (If no, ask) Where did you live mostly, then?

    c. How about your wife (husband)? Where did she live mostly?

4. Are you buying or do you rent this house?

5. What factors helped you to decide on moving to this neighborhood?

6. When you first moved into this neighborhood, did any of the neighbors call on you to welcome you to the neighborhood?

    (If yes, ask) Would you tell me about that?

7. When you first moved into the neighborhood, did any organized groups officially send visitors or come to see you?

    (If yes, ask) Would you tell me about this?

8. Is this the kind of neighborhood in which neighbors visit each other frequently?

    a. (If yes, ask) About how often do you visit your neighbors in their homes? (Check in appropriate space)

      __Daily

      __Frequently (once a week or more)

      __Occasionally (once a month or more)

      __Once a month or less

      __Only once

      __Never

    b. (If yes to 8) How often do your neighbors visit you in your home?

      __Daily

      __Frequently (once a week or more)

      __Occasionally (once a month or more)

      __Once a month or less

      __Only once

      __Never

9. Since you've lived here, have you noticed any change in the general attitude of your neighbors *toward you* since you first moved here?

    a. (If yes, ask) How do you think these attitudes have changed?

    b. (If yes to 9) Why do you think these attitudes have changed?

10. Have you ever experienced any hostility from any of your neighbors or shopkeepers in this area?

(If yes, ask) Would you care to describe this?

11. Since you've lived here, have you ever thought of moving away?

(If yes, ask) What made you think of this?

12. Now, I'm wondering about the groups you belong to. First, do you belong to any clubs or organizations located in this neighborhood?

(If no, skip to question 13).

(If yes, ask) What organizations are these?

(For each organization mentioned, ask) How did you happen to join that organization?

How about your wife? What organizations in this area does she belong to?

*13. (If no to 12, ask) Are there any special reasons why you haven't joined any local neighborhood groups?

14. Do you regularly attend a church located in this neighborhood?

a. (If yes, ask) Are you a member of this church?

b. How did you happen to start with this church?

15. In your search for housing, before moving to this neighborhood, did you have occasion to visit any community agency for assistance?

(If respondent doesn't understand, give example: i.e. UGN agency.)

(If yes, ask) Would you mind telling me about that?

16. "Now let's turn to some different questions. First, do you have any children living at home who are now under 21?"

(If no, skip to question 17)

(If yes, ask) How many girls, and what are their ages? ___, ___, ___, How many boys, and what are their ages? ___, ___, ___.

a. (If yes) Do any of your children (under 21 and over 5 only) belong to organizations or clubs which are located in this neighborhood?

b. (If no, ask) Can you tell me why they haven't joined any neighborhood clubs?

c. (If yes, ask) How about your oldest child (under 21)?

What neighborhood groups does he (she) belong to?
How did he (she) happen to join?
What about the second oldest child? What neighborhood groups does he (she) belong to? How did he (she) join?
(Repeat for other children.)

d. Would you say that most of the organizations that your children belong to are located right here in this neighborhood, or are they located mostly outside the neighborhood?

"Now let's turn to something different."

Suppose for a while that a good friend of yours has been offered an opportunity to move into this neighborhood. Let's say he doesn't know anything about the neighborhood or about the people who live here. He's interested in finding out something about the different kinds of people who live here, how they get along together, and how he'll like them. So he asks you:

17. What are the people in this neighborhood like?
    *(Probe in detail)
    Can you tell me more?
    (Probe) Are there any different kinds of people living in this neighborhood who are not like the ones you've just mentioned?

17a. Are there any Negro families living in this neighborhood?
    (If yes, skip to question 18)
    *(If no, or don't know, and respondent does not live immediately adjacent to Negro family, ask sequence beginning 17b., then terminate)
    *(If no or don't know, and respondent DOES live immediately adjacent to Negro family, say:) "We have already interviewed the _____ family who live _____. When they told us they were Negroes, we said we would not interview their neighbors without their consent. They said they would not mind our talking to their neighbors about them. So may we ask you a few questions about the family? Remember, everything you say is held by us strictly confidential.
    (If yes, go on with question 18)
    (If no, turn page, ask sequence, then terminate)

If no or don't know about Negro family

17b. (If not immediate neighbors, ask) What do you think *might* happen if a Negro family were to move into this neighborhood?

"Now before I leave, I'd like to ask you a couple of questions about yourself." (Skip to questions 38-41)

18. When did the family move into the neighborhood?
    *a. Then they were here when you moved in?
        (If yes to a., ask) What was your thinking about this?
    *b. Then you were here before they came?
        (If yes to b., ask) Were you or any members of your family concerned about this when they moved in? What was your thinking?
19. How did you happen to learn of their moving into the neighborhood?
20. When the family moved in, do you know if any of the neighbors were concerned about this?
    a. (If yes) What were they concerned about?
    b. (If yes) How did you learn of the neighbor's concern?
    c. (If yes) Was there any organized activity among the neighbors about this?
        (If yes to c., ask) Would you tell me about this?
    d. Other than the local neighbors, do you know of any organized groups in the neighborhood or from outside the neighborhood that became active when the colored family moved in?
        (If yes) Would you tell me about this? (Probe)

"Now let's turn to a different topic. I have here a list of community agencies located in Seattle." (Hand list to respondent)

21. Were any of these agencies involved in neighborhood affairs concerning the colored family?
    *(If no or don't know, turn page and go to question 25)
    a. *(If yes ask) What are these agencies?
    b. *(For each agency identified, check below and ask) How was that agency involved? What did they do?

c. *(For each agency identified also ask) Did you personally have contact with that agency or representative of
that agency? Would you tell about that?

List of Agencies Involved in Neighborhood Affairs

___Home Builder's Association of Greater Seattle
___Labor union organizations
___Local Citizen's Council on Improvement Association
___Local church
___Local police
___State Board Against Discrimination
___Businessmen's Club: such as Chamber of Commerce,
      Merchant's Association, Rotary
___Local Service Organizations: such as Eagles, Eastern
      Star, Kiwanis, Elks, Lions, Masons
___Seattle Housing Authority
___Social Agencies: such as State Department of Public
      Assistance (Welfare Dept.), Family Service Society
___Local public schools
___Parent-Teacher Association
___Real Estate Board
___Civic Unity Comm.
___United Good Neighbors
___Youth Groups: such as Boy Scouts, Campfire Girls,
      YMCA, YWCA
___National Association for Advancement of Colored
      Peoples (NAACP)
___Anti-Defamation League of B'nai B'rith
___Christian Friends for Racial Equality

22. How do you feel about agencies taking part in situations such
as this? (Probe) Would you tell me more about that? (Evalu-
ate feeling, and check in space)
      ___Very favorable
      ___Favorable
      ___Neither favorable nor unfavorable
      ___Unfavorable
      ___Very unfavorable
      (Probe: Then you feel _____ about this?)

23. Can you think of anything that such agencies can do that would be effective in relieving tensions or conflicts that might occur?

24. Are there any agencies not on this list which have been involved in neighborhood affairs concerning the Negro family?
   (If yes) What agencies are these? (For each agency mentioned, ask,) What did they do?

25. What do you think the people living in the neighborhood *should* do when a colored family moves in?

26. I'm wondering about this particular colored family. What are they like? (Don't know, go on to question 27.)
   Can you tell me more about them?
   a. Are they pretty much the same as the white people who live around here or are they different? (Check proper category and ask probe questions if needed)
   ___Don't know (go on to question 27)
   ___Same (then ask,) Are there *any* ways in which they are different?
   ___Different (then ask,) How are they different?

27. In general, how do you feel about having the colored family as neighbors?
   ___Very friendly
   ___Friendly
   ___Neither friendly nor unfriendly
   ___Unfriendly
   ___Very unfriendly
   (Probe: Then you feel _____ about them?)

28. Have you ever visited them in their home?
   a. (If yes, ask) How often do you visit them?
   ___Regularly (daily)
   ___Frequently (once a week or more)
   ___Occasionally (once a month or more)
   ___Once a month or less
   ___Rarely (once a year or less)
   ___Only once

29. Have they ever visited you in your home?
   a. (If yes, ask) How often do they visit you here?
   ___Regularly (daily)
   ___Frequently (once a week or more)

___Occasionally (once a month or more)

___Once a month or less

___Rarely (once a year or less)

___Only once

*b. Who does most of the visiting, Mr. or Mrs.?

30. *(If visiting occurs with the colored family ask,) How did these visits begin?

(If the respondent has children, ask) (If not, skip to #33)

31. Does the colored family have any children?

(If yes, ask) As far as you know, how many girls are there and what are their ages? ___, ___, ___, ___.

How many boys do they have, and how old are they about? ___, ___, ___.

32. Do your children ever play together with the colored family's children?

(If yes,) How often do they play together in your home?

___Every day

___Once a week or more

___Once a month or more

___Less than once a month

___Only once

(Probe:) Would you say they played here _____?

(If yes,) How often do they play together in the colored family's home?

___Every day

___Once a week or more

___Once a month or more

___Less than once a month

___Only once

(Probe:) Would you say they played there _____?

33. *Now there are a few other things before I finish. How do you think the other neighbors feel about having the colored family as neighbors?

___Very happy to have them

___Happy to have them

___Neither happy nor opposed to having them

___Opposed to having them

___Very opposed to having them

34. Do you know of any white families in this neighborhood who

moved out directly because of the colored family moving into this area?

(If yes) What happened?

35. How do you feel the colored family's presence here has influenced the value of the neighborhood property?

(Probe:) Why do you feel this way?

36. Do you know if the colored family has made any improvements in their property since they moved into the neighborhood?

(If yes, ask) What type of improvements have they made?

37. In your opinion, have they kept up the appearance of their property since they moved into the neighborhood?

"Now before I leave, I'd like to ask you a couple of questions about yourself."

38. What is your occupation?

Does your wife work? What does she do?

39. What are your ages? Husband's _____ Wife's _____

40. (Hand respondent income category card.) In what income category would you place yourself? How about your wife?

a.___Under $2000 annually	f.___$6000 – 6999
b.___$2000 – 2999	g.___$7000 – 7999
c.___$3000 – 3999	h.___$8000 – 8999
d.___$4000 – 4999	i.___$9000 – 9999
e.___$5000 – 5999	j.___$10,000 – 14,000
	k.___Over $14,000

41. What is the last school year you completed? How about your wife?

"Now I would like to express my appreciation to you and your family for your help in this study. Thank you very much."

NOTE: Edit your recorded data to be sure it's readable!

Time interview took: _____ minutes
Respondent's address: _____ _____ _____
Distance from Negro family __ blocks
General Comments:

Appendix B

METHODS FOR THE SELECTION OF THE SIX CASES REPORTED IN THIS STUDY

Two indexes were computed for each neighborhood, based on the responses of the Negro and five white neighbors: Ease of Entry Score, and Acceptance Score.

The Ease of Entry Score contained four items which contributed one point each to the final total: (1) Whether there was evidence in the cluster of interviews that the Negro newcomer was visited by his neighbors or (2) by the official visitors of an organized local group when he first moved into his home; (3) whether the Negro family was visited officially at some later time; (4) whether persons living in the neighborhood actively helped the Negro family to secure the house—this might be by the former owner or another person living nearby. These four plus points might be canceled by four minus points which were scored for evidence of neighborhood opposition to the Negro entry. The statement by the Negro or his neighbors that there was "opposition" scored one minus point; another minus was assigned to evidence of "organized opposition," a third to "hostility" on the part of shopkeepers, and a fourth to the statement of the Negro newcomer that he felt the need for the help of a social agency in order to secure the home. It should be noted that plus or minus scores were awarded only for actions that helped or hindered the entry. Zero scores were assigned for lack of visitation, lack of opposition, lack of requests for agency help. Mathematically, the score for Ease of Entry could range from minus four to plus four. In our sample of fifteen neighborhoods, this score ranged from minus two to plus three.

The Acceptance Score was based on six items which could be rated either plus or minus. The score includes both attitudinal and behavior items. Two points were added for statements by the Negro newcomer that opposition had lessened (persisted or increased) since his entry; and that he would be welcomed (or not welcomed) by others if he were to join a local neighborhood group. All residents were asked to estimate "whether you have noticed a change in the general attitude of your neighbors *toward you* since you first moved here." For the whites, this preceded any race-related questions. An estimate of continued "friendly" attitudes or "changes for the better" were scored plus one on the Acceptance Score. An estimate of "stayed poor" or "changed for the worse" were given minus one. Three points on the Acceptance Score were based on averages computed from answers of the white neighbors. The usual visitation patterns among neighbors were secured from questions early in the interview asking how often the respondent visited his neighbors in their homes and how often these visits were returned. Thus a neighborhood average could be computed. This neighborhood average was then compared with statements about interracial visitation which was secured from both Negro and white respondents. If the interracial visitation was at or above the level of general neighborhood visitation, one point was added to the Acceptance Score. If the interracial visitation was less than the level of general neighborhood visitation, one minus point was added on the Acceptance Index. A similar procedure was utilized in the assessment of statements of membership in local churches, PTA's, and other neighborhood clubs. The number of memberships of the Negro respondent was determined and then compared with the average number of memberships of white residents of the neighborhood. If the number of memberships of the Negro respondent was at or above the neighborhood average, then a point was added to the Acceptance Score. If it was below the neighborhood average, then a point was subtracted.

Finally, a numerical score was given to each of the alternatives to a question asked of white residents:

In general, how do you feel about having the colored family as neighbors? (Very friendly, friendly, neither friendly nor unfriendly, unfriendly, or very unfriendly)

If most respondents checked "very friendly" or "friendly," one point was added to the Acceptance Score. One point was subtracted if the answers indicated "unfriendly" or "very unfriendly."

Mathematically, the total on the Acceptance Score could range from minus six to plus six. Estimates could be made for only fourteen of the neighborhoods, since one Negro newcomer had arrived only two weeks before the interview. The actual range between Ease of Entry and Acceptance Scores was from minus two to plus six (case 8). Table 5 below shows the value of the two indexes for the fourteen neighborhoods. The six cases reported in the study head the list.

TABLE 5

Total on the Ease of Entry Score and the
Acceptance Score for Fourteen Neighborhoods

Neighborhood Identification	Ease of Entry Score	Acceptance Score
1	+2	+2
2	+3	+6
3	+2	+4
4	−1	0
5	0	+1
6	−1	0
7	−1	−1
8	−2	+6
9	0	+3
10	0	+1
11	+1	+6
12	+1	+5
13	+2	+3
14	0	0

Notes

INTRODUCTION

1. The authors wish to acknowledge the substantial help given to them by Reuel Seeman Amdur, whose Master's thesis concerned many of the questions dealt with in this book. See his "An Exploratory Study of Nineteen Negro Families in the Seattle Area Who Were First Negro Residents in White Neighborhoods, of Their White Neighbors, and of the Integration Process, Together with a Proposed Program to Promote Integration in Seattle" (M.S.W. thesis, University of Washington, 1962).

2. Throughout the study, the pioneer families will be referred to, on occasion, as "first *Negro* residents," "*Negro* couple," "*Negro* newcomers," and so forth. It should be noted, however, that three of the pioneer families involve interracial marriages, where one spouse is Caucasian. Thus, the term "Negro" is not an entirely accurate characterization of the couple. Race descriptions, in general, are imprecise, and it is unfortunate that another term, which would have had more precision and clarity, could not have been used. Only one of the fifteen basic clusters of interviews in a neighborhood contained an interracial couple. No white respondents expressed difficulty in identifying the pioneer family as a "Negro" family.

3. See questions 18-37 on pp. 100-4 in Appendix A.

4. See pp. 60-62 for a brief statement of methods used in analyzing social agency records.

5. Ernest A. T. Barth, *Case Studies in the Process of Integration in Neighborhoods of Seattle* (Seattle, Wash.: Greater Seattle Housing Council, 1960). In this study a tandem of interviewers, one representing the "real estate point of view" and the other the "human relations point of view," jointly interviewed families but independently recorded their answers. Almost complete agreement in the independent recordings demonstrated that one trained interviewer was sufficiently accurate to dispense with the tandem process. The pretest also showed that there

was relatively little disagreement among the cluster of six respondents in accounts of neighborhood association and climate of opinion, and that variations in the accounts supplemented and enriched the total narrative.

6. E. Franklin Frazier, *Black Bourgeoisie* (Glencoe, Ill.: Free Press, 1957).

7. Ernest A. T. Barth and Walter B. Watson, "Changing Negro-White Relations in the United States: An Analysis and Interpretation," *Sociologiske Meddeleser,* IX (1964).

CHAPTER ONE

1. Seattle's foreign-born white population numbered 59,720 in 1960, about 11 per cent of the total population. Another declining minority are the Japanese. In 1930, they were Seattle's largest minority with 8,448 persons as compared with 3,303 Negroes. Unless otherwise noted, population statistics in this report are taken from U.S. Bureau of the Census publications, Bulletin P-D 51 for the year 1950, and Final Report PHC (1)—142 for the year 1960. See also the detailed analysis of this question by Calvin F. Schmid and Wayne W. McVey, Jr., *Growth and Distribution of Minority Races in Seattle, Washington* (Seattle, Wash.: Seattle Public Schools, 1964).

2. The residue of growth is the increment in population size between any two time periods. In 1950 the population of the Seattle area was 524,875 and in 1960 it was 557,087. Thus the residue of growth was 32,212 persons. During this period, Seattle expanded its city boundaries, acquiring through the annexation a largely white population. Thus, the estimate of the contribution of the nonwhite minority to the residue of growth is understated. If there had been no annexations, the number of whites living in Seattle would have declined during the decade.

3. See the study by Calvin F. Schmid and Vincent A. Miller, *Impact of Recent Negro Migration on Seattle Schools* (Office of Population Research, University of Washington, 1959). A summary of the study is found in an article by E. B. Fussell in the Seattle *Times,* March 15, 1961.

4. The analysis in this paragraph and the one that follows was performed with the help of Walter Watson of the University of Washington.

5. Further information about the interracial climate of opinion according to surveys and polls is reported in the concluding chapter.

6. Murray Morgan, *Skid Road, an Informal Portrait of Seattle* (New York: Viking Press, 1962). See especially pp. 11-57. The Indians were conquered by alcohol and disease as well as the white man's guns.

7. Bob Karolevitz, "The Pacific Northwest's Own George Washington," Seattle *Times,* Feb. 16, 1964, "Charmed Land" Supplement, p. 2.

8. Morgan, *Skid Road,* pp. 67-106. Further details are included in Harvey O'Connor, *Revolution in Seattle, a Memoir* (New York: Monthly Review Press, 1964), p. 8ff.

9. Jacobus tenBroeck, Edward N. Barnhart, and Floyd W. Matson, *Prejudice, War, and the Constitution* (Berkeley and Los Angeles: University of California Press, 1954); Leonard Bloom and Ruth Riemer, *Removal and Return: The Socio-Economic Effects of the War on Japanese Americans* (Berkeley and Los Angeles: University of California Press, 1949); Alexander Leighton, *The Governing of Men* (Princeton, N.J.: Princeton University Press, 1945).

10. United States Army Western Defense Command and Fourth Army, Japanese in the United States, Final Report, *Japanese Evacuation from the West Coast* (Washington, D.C.: Government Printing Office, 1943), pp. 33-34.

11. Bloom and Riemer, *Removal and Return,* chapter 5.

12. Schmid and McVey, *Growth and Distribution,* p. 15.

13. Arval A. Morris and Daniel B. Ritter, "Racial Minority Housing in Washington," *Washington Law Review,* XXXVII, No. 2 (1962), 131-51.

14. National Committee Against Discrimination in Housing, "New Fair Housing Law in Mid- and Far-West: Defeats in Seattle and Tacoma," *Trends in Housing,* VIII, No. 1 (January-February, 1964), 1.

CHAPTER THREE

1. In this instance, "neighborhood" is defined as the census tract in which the pioneer family resides. Tract data are found in *U.S. Bureau of the Census, U.S. Censuses of Population and Housing: 1960, Census Tracts, Seattle, Washington,* Final Report PHC (1) —142.

2. The median family income of nonwhites living in the ten most densely populated nonwhite census tracts in 1960 was $5,562 according to the U.S. Census. This is about $4,000 less than the income reported by "pioneers" one year later. The estimates of family income for Negro families were made by the respondent at the time of the interview.

3. Amdur's thesis deals extensively with the Negro pioneer as a "marginal man." See above, p. 109. The evidence suggests that the pioneer families in our sample were at home in both white and Negro communities. In this sense, they are "marginal" to both. Following Seeman's lead, the authors hold that substantial good may flow from marginality. See Melvin Seeman, "Intellectual Perspective and Adjustment to Minority Status," *Social Problems* (January, 1956), pp. 142-53.

For a clear statement of the concept of "minority community," see E. A. Suchman, L. Dean, and R. Johnson, *Desegregation: Some Propositions and Research Suggestions* (Seattle, Wash.: Anti-Defamation League of B'nai B'rith, 1958), pp. 67-76.

CHAPTER FOUR

1. Two basically different approaches have been employed for the analysis of the housing transaction. One approach stresses the impersonal, economic, ecological processes by which an area undergoes change; the second takes up, one by one, the decisions that are made in the process—it is concerned with decision-making. The Chicago sociologists, Wirth and Cressey, have described most adequately the theory of ghetto formation as the inevitable end product of a succession of stages. This theory is shown by Wallace to be a variant of the economic "trickle-down" theory, which, by itself, is inadequate for explaining the succession phenomenon. For amplification of this approach, see the following: Paul F. Cressey, "The Succession of Cultural Groups" (Ph.D. thesis, University of Chicago, 1930); Louis Wirth, *The Ghetto* (Chicago: University of Chicago Press, 1928); David A. Wallace, "Residential Concentration of Negroes in Chicago" (Ph.D. thesis, Harvard University, 1953).

Corporate practices that characterize the decision-making approach are adequately described by Abrams and McEntire. See Charles Abrams, *Forbidden Neighbors* (New York: Harper and Brothers, 1955) and Davis McEntire, *Residence and Race* (Berkeley: University of California Press, 1960). The personal decisions that affect moving are dealt with in Peter Rossi's, *Why Families Move* (Glencoe, Ill.: Free Press, 1955) and *Housing Choices and Housing Constraints,* by N. N. Foote, J. Abu-Lughod, M. M. Foley, and L. Winnick (New York: McGraw-Hill, 1960). See especially chapters 6 and 7, "The Consumer Votes by Moving," p. 134-214.

2. One couple advertised in the newspaper for a house to rent, stating that they were an interracial couple. A white real estate man who believes in integration read their ad and helped them to find the housing they required.

3. There have been many adequate analyses of the role of the real estate industry in curtailing the flow of housing for Negroes. Abrams and McEntire deal with this adequately. See also United States Commission on Civil Rights, *Housing* (Washington, D.C.: Government Printing Office, 1961).

Empirical research by Stuart H. Palmer describes in detail the "gatekeeper" function of realtors. See Palmer, "The Role of the Real Estate Agent in the Structuring of Residential Areas: A Study in Social Control" (Ph.D. thesis, Yale University, 1955). Donald H. Bouma shows how the real estate board exercises power to control community housing decisions. See Bouma, "Analysis of the Social Power Position of a Real Estate Board," *Social Problems*, X, No. 2 (Fall, 1962), 121-32.

4. The quotations cited in this paragraph are taken from tape recordings of the hearings of the Mayor's Advisory Committee on Minority Housing, Seattle, Wash., Oct. 19, 1962.

5. The history of the activities of the Real Estate Board with respect to minority housing is not complete without specific mention of their part in the Greater Seattle Housing Council. This is a coordinating group, receiving staff services from the Executive Director of Seattle Civic Unity, which includes in its membership the Board, other organizations in public and private housing, human relations, community planning and social services, church groups, and the like. Although its major purpose has been to promote research about minority housing, it has also conducted educational meetings to better interracial relations in housing. Most recently it has encouraged the establishment of a housing listing service for minorities. Two chairmen of the Greater Seattle Housing Council have concurrently been chairmen of the Real Estate Board.

6. Ernest A. T. Barth, *Case Studies on the Process of Integration in Neighborhoods of Seattle, Washington* (Seattle, Wash.: Greater Seattle Housing Council, 1960), p. 27.

CHAPTER FIVE

1. There are exceptions to this statement. Recently a fifteen-pound rock was thrown through the picture window of a Negro newcomer to Lake Forest Park, a suburb of Seattle. Another pioneer couple sold their home because of unfriendly, threatening attitudes. In another case the front window of a pioneer home was broken by a shotgun blast. These episodes occurred after data collection had been terminated. Also, there have been recurring incidents of interracial violence in Seattle's Central Area: knifings, gang fights, police brutality.

2. It should be noted that the fifteen neighborhoods have a history of stability: about one third of the respondents had lived in their present homes over ten years, some as long as thirty-four, thirty-six, thirty-nine, and forty-two years. Another third had been there five to ten years, and the balance a lesser period. Apparently the advent of the Negro newcomers has not drastically disturbed the continuing stability of these neighborhoods.

3. Only one of the fifteen clusters of interviews involves an interracial marriage. In fourteen neighborhoods both husband and wife in the pio-

neer family identify themselves as Negro. Two other interracial couples were interviewed during the study, but no companion interviews with white neighbors were collected.

CHAPTER SIX

1. Two somewhat different discussions of the neighborhood integration process as it pertains to Negro families are found in Amdur and Tillman. Reuel S. Amdur, "An Exploratory Study of Nineteen Negro Families" (M.S.W. thesis, University of Washington, 1962), pp. 96-112. James A. Tillman, Jr., "Morningtown, U.S.A.—A Composite Case History of Neighborhood Change," *Journal of Intergroup Relations,* II (Spring, 1961), 156-66. See also Eleanor P. Wolf, "The Invasion-Succession Sequence as a Self-Fulfilling Prophesy," *Journal of Social Issues,* XIII (1957), 19-20.

2. The Deerfield incident in Illinois set off a discussion of the advantages and disadvantages of polling a neighborhood to see how residents felt about the advent of Negroes. Although there is almost unanimous rejection of polls as a means of decision-making with respect to whether a Negro should be allowed to move into a hitherto white area, there is, nevertheless, wide difference in opinion among human relations practitioners on the value of advanced preparation of a neighborhood for its first Negro family. Northwood and Klein found that a sample of 138 officials and practitioners of housing, traditional social work, and human relations agencies split in half: sixty-nine thought that educational campaigns just before the Negro entry were "desirable," and sixty-nine thought they were not. See L. K. Northwood and Louise H. Klein, "The Benign Quota, an Unresolved Issue of Attitudes of Agency Personnel," *Phylon,* XXV, No. 2 (Summer, 1964), 111.

3. In three neighborhoods, no such test could be made. In one, either no residents were interviewed who lived there at the time of the entry or they did not know of the presence of the Negro. In another, the pioneers had moved during the past month; hence, there was little data on the integration process. In the last case, some data were ambiguous or contradictory on relevant points.

4. Quite a number of studies have been directed toward the contact theory of improving interracial attitudes. See Muzafer Sherif, "Superordinate Goals in the Reduction of Intergroup Conflicts," *American Journal of Sociology* (January, 1958); Morton Deutsch and Mary E. Collins, *Interracial Housing: A Psychological Evaluation of a Social Experiment* (Minneapolis: University of Minnesota Press, 1951); D. M. Wilner, R. P. Walkey, and S. W. Cook, *Human Relations in Interracial Housing* (Minneapolis: University of Minnesota Press, 1955); Information and Education Division, U.S. War Department, "Opinions about

Negro Infantry Platoons in White Companies of Seven Divisions," in *Readings in Social Psychology*, ed. T. M. Newcomb and E. L. Hartley (New York: Henry Holt, 1947), pp. 542-46. For a critique of this theory, see Hans B. C. Spiegel, "Tenants' Intergroup Attitudes in a Public Housing Project with Declining White Population," *Phylon*, XXI (Spring, 1960), 30-39.

5. The findings of these sections accord with those of Fellin and Litwak that neighborhood integration of recent newcomers (Caucasians in their study) was facilitated where the newcomer was prepared "psychologically" for the change, and where he was greeted and accepted by local voluntary organizations. Phillip Fellin and Eugene Litwak, "Neighborhood Cohesion under Conditions of Mobility," *American Sociological Review*, XXVIII, No. 3 (June, 1963), 364-76.

CHAPTER SEVEN

1. The authors are indebted to careful analysis given this topic by Frances Rideout Coughlin in her paper, "A Conceptual Scheme for the Analysis of the Work of Intergroup Agencies" (University of Washington School of Social Work, June, 1962, mimeographed paper).

2. It could be argued that the Negro family's report might be inaccurate about agency activities and visits. However, in some instances these visits and activities were verified from records of the agencies and from accounts of the professional workers.

3. Charlotte Donaldson and George Ferguson, "Progress Report on an Exploratory Survey of the Differentiation of Function and Role of Human Relations Agencies and their Interaction" (University of Washington, M.S.W. group thesis, 1961).

4. The minutes of the NAACP were not analyzed.

5. The King County Intergroup Relations Council is an association of professional workers (and a few key community leaders) in the human relations agencies in the area. There was no Seattle chapter of the Congress on Racial Equality at the time the field work for this study was carried out.

6. Ernest A. T. Barth, "The Causes and Consequences of Interagency Conflict," *Sociological Inquiry*, XXXIII, No. 1 (Winter, 1963), 51-56. See also Milton M. Gordon, "Social Structure and Goals in Group Relations," in *Freedom of Control in Modern Society*, ed. M. Berger, T. Abel, and C. H. Page (New York: Van Nostrand, 1954).

CHAPTER EIGHT

1. For the best general discussions of the subject, see: Gordon W. Allport, *The Nature of Prejudice* (New York: Doubleday, 1958); Donald L.

Noel, "Correlates of Anti-White Prejudice: Attitudes of Negroes in Four American Cities" (Ph.D. thesis, Cornell University, 1961). The present work probably draws most heavily on *Prejudice and Society* by Earl Raab and Seymour M. Lipset (New York: Anti-Defamation League of B'nai B'rith, 1959). For popular pamphlets on the subject, see: A. D. Black, *Who's My Neighbor?* (Public Affairs Pamphlet No. 273, October, 1958); Race Relations Department, American Missionary Association, *If Your Next Neighbors Are Negroes,* Nashville, Tenn., 1951; American Jewish Congress, *The Myths of Racial Integration,* New York, n.d.

2. Laurenti, "Effects of Nonwhite Purchases on Market Prices of Residences," *Appraisal Journal,* XX (July, 1952), 314-29; Belden Morgan, "Values in Transition Areas: Some New Concepts," *Review of the Society of Residential Appraisers,* XVIII (March, 1952), 5-10.

3. Mayor's Commission on Group Relations, *Newark, A City in Transition* (Newark, N.J., 1959), Vol. 2, book 1, pp. 20ff.

4. L. K. Northwood, "The Threat and Potential of Urban Renewal," *Journal of Intergroup Relations,* II (Spring, 1961), 101-14; Martin Millspaugh and Gurney Breckenfeld, *The Human Side of Urban Renewal* (New York: Ives Washburn, Inc., 1960). E. Rutledge and W. R. Valentine, "Urban Renewal Planning for Balanced Communities," *Journal of Intergroup Relations,* I (Winter, 1960-61).

Even textbooks are thoroughly inadequate in the treatment of this question. See Lloyd Marcus, *The Treatment of Minorities in Secondary School Textbooks* (New York: Anti-Defamation League of B'nai B'rith, 1961).

5. For exception to newspaper sensationalism, see: R. Bass, "Prejudice Won't Make Us Sell *Our* House," *Coronet* (July, 1959); W. Peters, "Who Chooses the People You Know?" *Redbook* (June, 1959).

6. Elizabeth Heim, "A Study of the Adjustment Problems of Negro Families Who Have Settled in White Neighborhoods in the Pittsburgh Area, and the Attitudes of Their White Neighbors" (unpublished tutorial study, Chatham College, Pittsburgh, April 20, 1959).

7. Chester L. Hunt, *Research Report on Integrated Housing in Kalamazoo* (Kalamazoo, Mich.: W. E. Upjohn Institute for Community Research, July, 1959).

8. Henry G. Stetler, *Racial Integration in Private Residential Neighborhoods in Connecticut* (Hartford, Conn.: Commission on Civil Rights, 1957).

9. Anne Braden, *The Wall Between* (New York: Monthly Review Press, 1958); Marvin Bressler, "The Myers' Case: An Instance of Successful Racial Invasion," *Social Problems,* VIII (Fall, 1960), 126-42; Eunice Grier and George Grier, *Privately Developed Interracial Hous-*

ing (Berkeley and Los Angeles: University of California Press, 1960); Richard K. Kerckhoff, "A Study of Racially Changing Neighbors," *Merrill-Palmer Quarterly*, No. 3 (Fall, 1957), pp. 15-49; Sophia M. Robison, John A. Morsell, and Edna A. Merson, *Summary of Survey on Country-Wide Instances of Open Occupancy Housing* (New York: Committee on Civil Rights in Manhattan, Inc., 1957).

10. Davis McEntire, *Residence and Race* (Berkeley and Los Angeles: University of California Press, 1960).

11. The best general work that deals with ameliorative efforts is J. P. Dean and A. Rosen, *A Manual of Intergroup Relations* (Chicago: University of Chicago Press, 1955). Many of the intergroup programs have been evaluated through empirical research. For a comprehensive review of these studies, see C. Selltiz, M. Jahoda, M. Deutsch, and S .W. Cook, *Research Methods in Social Relations* (New York: Henry Holt, 1959). The Council on Social Work Education has prepared a case record for teaching purposes describing the work of an Urban League social worker in aid of an interracial pioneering couple: Subcommittee on Teaching Materials in Community Organization, *Racial Tensions in a Northern City* (New York: Council on Social Work Education, 1956). A practical manual on the subject, entitled *Fair Housing Handbook*, was prepared in 1964 by the American Friends Service Committee (160 N. 15th Street, Philadelphia), and the National Committee Against Discrimination in Housing (426 W. 58th Street, New York City).

12. A similar project, undertaken by the American Friends Service Committee on the basis of a door-to-door canvass, is reported in Ernest A. T. Barth and Sue March, "Research Note on the Subject of Minority Housing," *Journal of Intergroup Relations*, III, No. 4 (1962), 314-20.

13. This information was taken from the "Housing Workshop Summary" of a conference held in Seattle on March 9, 1963, under the auspices of the Seattle Urban League and the Central Brokers Association.

14. The information about these two organizations is derived largely from first-hand experience by the authors, from the newsletters and brochures of the two organizations, and from a special statement in writing and an interview with Sidney Gerber, secretary of the Fair Housing Listing Service and organizer of Harmony Homes, Inc.

15. *Newsletter of Harmony Homes, Inc.* (July, 1964).

16. Jack Rothman, "The Ghetto Makers," *Nation* (Oct. 7, 1961), pp. 222-25.

17. L. K. Northwood and Louise Klein, "The Benign Quota, an Unresolved Issue of Attitudes of Agency Personnel," *Phylon*, XXV, No. 2 (Summer, 1964), 109-22.

18. Seattle *Times,* July 28, 1963.

19. *Ibid.,* July 31, 1963.

20. *Newsletter of Harmony Homes, Inc.* (July, 1964).

21. Harold Goldblatt and F. Cromein, "The Effective Social Reach of the Fair Housing Practices Law of the City of New York," *Social Problems,* IX, No. 4 (Spring, 1962), 365-70; *Lawyers' Guild Review* (Special Issue on Integration in Housing), XVIII, No. 1 (Spring, 1958); Margaret Fisher and Frances Levenson, *Federal, State and Local Action Affecting Race and Housing* (New York: National Association of Intergroup Relations Officials, September, 1962); Charles Abrams, "The Housing Order and Its Limits," *Commentary* (January, 1963), pp. 10-14.

22. See "A Report to the Mayor and City Council of Chicago on the Present Status and Effectiveness of Existing Fair Housing Practices Legislation in the United States as of April 1, 1963," prepared by Clifford J. Campbell and Edward Marciniak (Chicago Commission on Human Relations, 1963).

23. Arval Morris and Daniel Ritter, "Racial Minority Housing in Washington," *Washington Law Review,* XXVII, No. 2 (1961), 131-51.

24. The U.S. Census data on which this analysis is based lumps together Negro with other nonwhite races. In Seattle, only 55 per cent of the nonwhite population in 1960 was Negro. Thus, comparisons of "Negro" pioneers with the nonwhite total is somewhat invalid. It tends to overstate the buying power of the Negro population. For current purposes the data are sufficiently precise to enable rough comparisons to be made. See U.S. Bureau of the Census, *U.S. Censuses of Population and Housing, 1960, Census Tracts, Seattle, Washington.*

25. Catherine Bauer, "Social Questions in Housing and Community Planning," *Journal of Social Issues,* VII (1951), 1-34. See especially 12ff. An excellent statement of the housing problem is found in Miles L. Colean, *Renewing Our Cities* (New York: Twentieth Century Fund, 1953). The race implications of the housing problem receive good treatment in E. C. Banfield and M. Grodzins, *Government and Housing in Metropolitan Areas* (New York: McGraw-Hill, 1958).

26. Claire Selltiz and Stuart W. Cook, "How People Feel and Act about Interracial Housing" (unpublished paper submitted to the Commission on Race and Housing, March, 1957).

27. *Ibid.*

28. H. H. Hyman and Paul B. Sheatsley, "Attitudes Toward Desegregation," *Scientific American,* CXCV, No. 6 (December, 1956). See also Gallup Poll in New York *Herald Tribune,* Oct. 17, 1958; only 18 per cent of white persons said they "definitely" would move if "a colored family came to live next door."

29. Keith S. Griffiths, *An Audit of Intergroup Relations in the City of Seattle* (Seattle, Wash.: Health and Welfare Council, 1950).

30. John S. Holley, "Pockets of Prejudice," *Frontier,* VIII (January, 1957), 16-17.

31. Jack Rothman, "The Ghetto Makers," *Nation* (Oct. 7, 1961), pp. 222-25.

32. Nelson Foote, J. Abu-Lughod, M. Foley, and L. Winnick, *Housing Choices and Housing Constraints* (New York: McGraw-Hill, 1960); Robert C. Weaver, "Class, Race and Urban Renewal," *Land Economics,* XXXVI, No. 3 (August, 1960), 235-51; Catherine Baker Wurster, "Framework for an Urban Society," in *Goals for Americans: The Report of the President's Commission on National Goals* (New York: Prentice-Hall, 1960); L. K. Northwood, "Social Work in the Amelioration of Social Problems in the Inner City, a First Step toward Defining a Small Area Approach" (University of Washington, School of Social Work, 1962); James A. Tillman, Jr., "Fair Housing: A Conceptual Frame of Reference," *Journal of Intergroup Relations,* I, No. 4 (Autumn, 1960).

Bibliography

BOOKS

Abrahamson, Julia. *A Neighborhood Finds Itself.* New York: Harper and Brothers, 1959.

Abrams, Charles. *Forbidden Neighbors.* New York: Harper and Brothers, 1955.

Allport, Gordon W. *The Nature of Prejudice.* Abridged ed.; Garden City, N.Y.: Doubleday, 1959.

Banfield, Edward C., and Morton Grodzins. *Government and Housing in Metropolitan Areas.* New York: McGraw-Hill, 1958.

Barron, Milton L. (ed.). *American Minorities.* New York: Alfred A. Knopf, 1958.

Bloom, Leonard, and Ruth Riemer. *Removal and Return: The Socio-Economic Effects of the War on Japanese Americans.* Berkeley and Los Angeles: University of California Press, 1949.

Braden, Anne. *The Wall Between.* New York: Monthly Review Press, 1958.

Cartwright, Dorwin, and Alvin Zander (ed.). *Group Dynamics.* Evanston, Ill., and White Plains, N.Y.: Row, Peterson and Company, 1953.

Colean, Miles L. *Renewing Our Cities.* New York: Twentieth Century Fund, 1953.

Conser, Eugene P. *Human Rights and the Realtor.* National Association of Real Estate Boards, 1963.

Dean, John P., and Alex Rosen. *A Manual of Intergroup Relations.* Phoenix ed.; Chicago: University of Chicago Press, 1963.

Deutsch, Morton, and Mary Evans Collins. *Interracial Housing: A Psychological Evaluation of a Social Experiment.* Minneapolis: University of Minnesota Press, 1951.

Foote, N. N., J. Abu-Lughod, M. M. Foley, and L. Winnick.

Housing Choices and Housing Constraints. New York: Mc-Graw-Hill, 1960.

Frazier, E. Franklin. *Black Bourgeoisie.* Glencoe, Ill.: Free Press, 1957.

Glazer, Nathan, and Davis McEntire (ed.). *Studies in Housing and Minority Groups.* Berkeley and Los Angeles: University of California Press, 1960.

Grier, Eunice, and George Grier. *Privately Developed Interracial Housing.* Berkeley and Los Angeles: University of California Press, 1960.

Hartley, Eugene L., and Ruth E. Hartley. *Fundamentals of Social Psychology.* New York: Alfred A. Knopf, 1958.

Homans, George C. *The Human Group.* New York: Harcourt, Brace and Company, 1950.

Laurenti, Luigi. *Property Values and Race.* Berkeley and Los Angeles: University of California Press, 1960.

Leighton, Alexander. *The Governing of Men.* Princeton, N.J.: Princeton University Press, 1945.

Lomax, Louis E. *The Negro Revolt.* New York: Signet Books, 1963.

McEntire, Davis. *Residence and Race.* Berkeley and Los Angeles: University of California Press, 1960.

Meyerson, Martin. *Housing, People and Cities.* New York: Mc-Graw-Hill, 1963.

Millspaugh, Martin, and Gurney Breckenfeld. *The Human Side of Urban Renewal.* New York: Ives Washburn, Inc., 1960.

Morgan, Murray. *Skid Road, An Informal Portrait of Seattle.* New York: Viking Press, 1962.

O'Connor, Harvey. *Revolution in Seattle, A Memoir.* New York: Monthly Review Press, 1964.

Rapkin, Chester, and William G. Grigsby. *The Demand for Housing in Racially Mixed Areas.* Berkeley and Los Angeles: University of California Press, 1960.

Redl, Fritz, and David Wineman. *The Aggressive Child.* Glencoe, Ill.: Free Press, 1957.

Robison, Sophia M., John A. Morsell, and Edna A. Merson. *Summary of Survey on Country-Wide Instances of Open Occupancy Housing.* New York: Committee on Civil Rights in Manhattan, Inc., 1957.

Rossi, Peter H. *Why Families Move.* Glencoe, Ill.: Free Press, 1955.

Selltiz, Claire, Marie Jahoda, Morton Deutsch, and Stuart W. Cook. *Research Methods in Social Relations.* New York: Henry Holt, 1959.

Simpson, George Eaton, and J. Milton Yinger. *Racial and Cultural Minorities.* New York: Harper and Brothers, 1958.

Straus, Nathan. *Two-Thirds of a Nation.* New York: Alfred A. Knopf, 1952.

tenBroek, Jacobus, Edward N. Barnhart, and Floyd W. Matson. *Prejudice, War, and the Constitution.* Berkeley and Los Angeles: University of California Press, 1954.

Williams, Robin M. *Strangers Next Door.* New York: Prentice-Hall, 1964.

Wilner, D. M., R. P. Walkey, and S. W. Cook. *Human Relations in Interracial Housing.* Minneapolis: University of Minnesota Press, 1955.

Wirth, Louis. *The Ghetto.* Chicago: University of Chicago Press, 1928.

ARTICLES

Abrams, Charles. "The Housing Order and Its Limits," *Commentary* (January, 1963), pp. 10-14.

Allport, Gordon W. "Prejudice: Is It Societal or Personal?" *Journal of Social Issues,* XVIII (1962), 120-34.

Anonymous. "Rock Hurled Through Negroes' Window," Seattle *Times,* Dec. 3, 1961, p. 16.

Associated Press. "Barking Dog Saves Family from Bomb," Seattle *Times,* Jan. 14, 1962, p. 1.

Barth, Ernest A. T. "The Causes and Consequences of Interagency Conflict," *Sociological Inquiry,* XXXIII, No. 1 (Winter, 1963), 51-56.

————, and Baha Abu-Laban. "Power Structure and the Negro Subcommunity," *American Sociological Review,* XXIV, No. 1 (February, 1959), 69-76.

Barth, Ernest A. T., and Sue March. "Research Note on the Subject of Minority Housing," *Journal of Intergroup Relations,* III, No. 4 (1962), 314-20.

Barth, Ernest A. T., and Walter B. Watson. "Changing Negro-White Relations in the United States: An Analysis and Interpretation," *Sociologiske Meddeleser,* IX (1964).

Bass, R. "Prejudice Won't Make Us Sell *Our* House," *Coronet* (July, 1959).

Bauer, Catherine. "Social Questions in Housing and Community Planning," *Journal of Social Issues,* VII (1951), 1-34.

Bell, Wendell, and Ernest M. Willis. "The Segregation of Negroes in American Cities: A Comparative Analysis," *Social and Economic Studies,* VI (March, 1957), 59-75.

Bouma, Donald H. "Analysis of the Social Power Position of a Real Estate Board," *Social Problems,* X, No. 2 (Fall, 1962), 121-32.

Bressler, Marvin. "The Myers' Case: An Instance of Successful Racial Invasion," *Social Problems,* VIII (Fall, 1960), 126-42.

Drake, St. Clair. "Should We Expect Newcomers to Conform," in *Welcoming Newcomers to Cities.* New York: National Federation of Settlements and Neighborhood Centers, 1963.

Ehrlich, Howard J. "The Study of Prejudice in American Social Science," *Journal of Intergroup Relations,* III (Spring, 1962), 117-25.

Erdman, Palmore, and John Howe. "Residential Integration and Property Values," *Social Problems,* X, No. 1 (Summer, 1962).

Fellin, Phillip, and Eugene Litwak. "Neighborhood Cohesion under Conditions of Mobility," *American Sociological Review,* XXVIII, No. 3 (June, 1963), 364-76.

Gans, Herbert J. "The Human Implications of Current Redevelopment and Relocation Planning," *Journal of the American Institute of Planners,* XXV, No. 1 (February, 1959), 15-25.

Goldblatt, Harold, and F. Cromein. "The Effective Social Reach of the Fair Housing Practices Law of the City of New York," *Social Problems,* IX, No. 4 (Spring, 1962), 365-70.

Gordon, Milton M. "Social Structure and Goals in Group Relations," in *Freedom of Control in Modern Society,* ed. M. Berger, T. Abel, and C. H. Page. New York: Van Nostrand, 1954.

Handlin, Oscar. "Historical Perspectives on the American Ethnic Group," *Daedalus,* XC, No. 2 (Spring, 1961), 220-32.

Holley, John S. "Pockets of Prejudice," *Frontier,* VIII (January, 1957), 16-17.

Hunt, Chester L. "A Research Report on Integration Housing in a Small Northern City," *Journal of Intergroup Relations,* III (Winter, 1961-62), 65-79.

————. "Private Integrated Housing in a Medium Size Northern City," *Social Problems,* VII (Winter, 1959-60), 196-209.

Horne, Frank S. "The Open City—Threshold to American Maturity," *Phylon,* XVIII, No. 2 (June, 1957), 133-39.

Hyman, H. H., and Paul B. Sheatsley. "Attitudes Toward Desegregation," *Scientific American,* CXCV, No. 6 (December, 1956).

Isaacs, Reginald R. "The Neighborhood Unit as an Instrument for Segregation," *Journal of Housing,* V, No. 8 (August, 1948), 215-19.

Karolevitz, Bob. "The Pacific Northwest's Own George Washington," Seattle *Times,* Feb. 16, 1964, "Charmed Land" Supplement, p. 2.

Kerckhoff, Richard K. "A Study of Racially Changing Neighbors," *Merrill-Palmer Quarterly,* No. 3 (Fall, 1957), 15-49.

Laurenti, Luigi. "Effects of Non-White Purchases on Market Prices of Residences," *Appraisal Journal,* XX (July, 1952), 314-29.

Lewis, Hylan, and Mozell Hill. "Desegregation, Integration, and the Negro Community," *Annals of the American Academy of Political and Social Science,* CCCIV (March, 1956), 116-23.

Linder, Leo J. "The Social Results of Segregation in Housing," *Lawyers' Guild Review,* XVIII (Spring, 1958), 2-11.

McGraw, B. T. "Urban Renewal," *Phylon,* XIX (Spring, 1958), 45-55.

Mayer, Albert J. "Race and Private Housing: A Social Problem and a Challenge to Understanding Human Behavior," *Journal of Social Issues,* XIII (1957), 3-6.

Merton, Robert K. "Discrimination and the American Creed," in Robert M. MacIver, *Discrimination and National Welfare.* New York: Harper and Brothers, 1949, pp. 99-124.

Miller, Alexander F. "Levittown U.S.A.," *Phylon,* XIX (Spring, 1958), 108-12.

Miller, Loren. "The Changing Metro-Urban Complex," *Journal of Intergroup Relations,* III (Winter, 1961-62), 55-64.

Montgomery, Dorothy S. "Relocation and Its Impact on Families," *Social Casework,* XLI, No. 8 (October, 1960), 402-7.

Morgan, Belden. "Values in Transition Areas: Some New Concepts," *Review of the Society of Residential Appraisers,* XVIII (March, 1952), 5-10.

Morris, Arval A., and Daniel B. Ritter. "Racial Minority Housing in Washington," *Washington Law Review,* XXXVII, No. 2 (1962), 131-51.

National Committee Against Discrimination in Housing. "New Fair Housing Law in Mid- and Far-West: Defeats in Seattle and Tacoma," *Trends in Housing,* VIII, No. 1 (January-February, 1964), 1.

Noren, Sonia. "Cruel Act," Seattle *Times,* Feb. 6, 1962, p. 8.

Northwood, L. K. "The Threat and Potential of Urban Renewal: A Workable Program for Better Race Relations," *Journal of Intergroup Relations,* II (Spring, 1961), 101-14.

————, and Louise H. Klein. "The Benign Quota, an Unresolved Issue of Attitudes of Agency Personnel," *Phylon,* XXV, No. 2 (Summer, 1964), 109-22.

Peters, W. "Who Chooses the People You Know?" *Redbook* (June, 1959).

Reynolds, Harry W., Jr. "Family Relocation Can Succeed in in Urban Renewal Work," *The American City* (April, 1960), pp. 183ff.

Rose, Arnold, and Leon Warshay. "The Adjustment of Migrants to Cities," *Social Forces,* XXXVI (October, 1957), 72-76.

Rothman, Jack. "The Ghetto Makers," *Nation,* CXCIII (Oct. 7, 1961), 222-25.

Rutledge, E., and W. R. Valentine. "Urban Renewal Planning for Balanced Communities," *Journal of Intergroup Relations,* I (Winter, 1960-61).

Seeman, Melvin, "Intellectual Perspective and Adjustment to Minority Status," *Social Problems* (January, 1956), pp. 142-53.

Sherif, Muzafer. "Superordinate Goals in the Reduction of Intergroup Conflicts," *American Journal of Sociology* (January, 1958).

Smith, Bulkeley, Jr. "The Differential Residential Segregation of Working-Class Negroes in New Haven," *American Sociological Review,* XXIV, No. 4 (August, 1959), 529-33.

Spiegel, Hans B. C. "Tenants' Intergroup Attitudes in a Public Housing Project with Declining White Population," *Phylon,* XXI (Spring, 1960), 30-39.

Sussman, Marvin B. "The Role of Neighborhood Associations in Private Housing for Racial Minorities," *Journal of Social Issues,* XIII, No. 4 (1957), 31-37.

Taeuber, Karl E., and Alma F. Taeuber. "The Negro as an Immigrant Group: Recent Trends in Racial and Ethnic Segregation in Chicago," *American Journal of Sociology,* LXIX, No. 4 (January, 1964), 374ff.

Tillman, James A., Jr. "Fair Housing: A Conceptual Frame of Reference," *Journal of Intergroup Relations,* I, No. 4 (Autumn, 1960).

———. "Morningtown, U.S.A.—A Composite Case History of Neighborhood Change," *Journal of Intergroup Relations,* II (Spring, 1961), 156-66.

United States War Department. Information and Education Division. "Opinions About Negro Infantry Platoons in White Companies of Seven Divisions," in *Readings in Social Psychology,* ed. T. M. Newcomb and E. L. Hartley. New York: Henry Holt, 1947.

Weaver, Robert C. "Class, Race and Urban Renewal," *Land Economics,* XXXVI, No. 3 (August, 1960), 235-61.

———. "Integration in Public and Private Housing," *Annals of the American Academy of Political and Social Science,* CCCIV (March, 1956), 86-97.

Westie, Frank R. "Negro-White Status Differentials and Social Distance," *American Sociological Review,* XVII (October, 1952), 550-58.

Wolf, Eleanor P. "The Invasion-Succession Sequence as a Self-Fulfilling Prophecy," *Journal of Social Issues,* XIII (1957), 7-20.

Wurster, Catherine Bauer. "Framework for an Urban Society," in *Goals for Americans, The Report of the President's Commission on National Goals.* New York: Prentice-Hall, 1960, pp. 225-48.

PAMPHLETS

Advance Mortgage Corporation. *Midwestern Minority Housing Markets.* Chicago, December 1, 1962.

American Friends Service Committee and National Committee Against Discrimination in Housing. *Fair Housing Handbook.* New York, 1964.

American Jewish Congress. *The Myths of Racial Integration.* New York, n.d.

American Missionary Association. Race Relations Department. *If Your Next Neighbors Are Negroes.* Nashville, Tenn., 1951.

Barth, Ernest A. T. *Case Studies of the Process of Integration in Neighborhoods of Seattle, Washington.* Seattle, Wash.: Greater Seattle Housing Council, 1960.

Black, A. D. *Who's My Neighbor?* Public Affairs Pamphlet No. 273 (October, 1958).

Commission on Race and Housing. *Where Shall We Live?* Berkeley and Los Angeles: University of California Press, 1958.

Fisher, Margaret, and Frances Levenson. *Federal, State and Local Action Affecting Race and Housing.* New York: National Association of Intergroup Relations Officials, 1962.

Griffiths, Keith S. *An Audit of Intergroup Relations in the City of Seattle.* Seattle, Wash.: Health and Welfare Council, 1950.

Hunt, Chester L. *Research Report on Integrated Housing in Kalamazoo.* Kalamazoo, Mich.: W. E. Upjohn Institute for Community Research, July, 1959.

Lawyers' Guild Review (Special Issue on Integration in Housing), XVIII, No. 1 (Spring, 1958).

Marcus, Lloyd. *The Treatment of Minorities in Secondary School Textbooks.* New York: Anti-Defamation League of B'nai B'rith, 1961.

Mayor's Commission on Group Relations. *Newark, A City in Transition.* Newark, N.J., 1959.

National Conference on Religion and Race. *Religion's Role in the Racial Crisis.* Chicago, 1963.

National Urban League. *Racial Bias and Housing.* New York, 1963.

New Jersey Division on Civil Rights. *Open Doors.* Trenton, N.J.: New Jersey State Board Against Discrimination, 1964.

Raab, Earl, and Seymour Martin Lipset. *Prejudice and Society.* New York: Anti-Defamation League of B'nai B'rith, 1959.

Schmid, Calvin F., and Wayne W. McVey, Jr. *Growth and Distribution of Minority Races in Seattle, Washington.* Seattle, Wash.: Seattle Public Schools, 1964.

Schmid, Calvin F., and Vincent A. Miller. *Impact of Recent Negro Migration on Seattle Schools.* Seattle, Wash.: Office of

Population Research, University of Washington, 1959.

Seattle Public Schools. *The Report of the Citizens' Advisory Committee for Equal Educational Opportunity.* Seattle, Wash., 1964.

Stetler, Henry. *Racial Integration in Private Residential Neighborhoods in Connecticut.* Hartford, Conn.: Commission on Civil Rights, 1957.

Subcommittee on Teaching Materials in Community Organization. *Racial Tensions in a Northern City.* New York: Council on Social Work Education, 1956.

Suchman, E. A., L. Dean, and R. Johnson. *Desegregation: Some Propositions and Research Suggestions.* Seattle, Wash.: Anti-Defamation League of B'nai B'rith, 1958.

Thomas, Trevor. *San Francisco's Housing Market—Open or Closed.* San Francisco, Calif.: Council for Civic Unity, 1960.

United States Commission on Civil Rights. *Housing.* Washington, D.C.: Government Printing Office, 1961.

United States Housing and Home Finance Agency. *Equal Opportunity in Housing.* San Francisco, Calif.: Housing and Home Finance Agency, Region VI, 1964.

Watson, Walter B. *Seattle's Negro Population, A Statistical Profile, 1963.* Seattle, Wash.: Seattle Urban League Annual Report, 1964.

UNPUBLISHED SOURCES

Amdur, Reuel Seeman. "An Exploratory Study of Nineteen Negro Families in the Seattle Area Who Were First Negro Residents in White Neighborhoods, of Their White Neighbors, and of the Integration Process, Together with a Proposed Program to Promote Integration in Seattle." Unpublished M.S.W. thesis, University of Washington, 1962.

Campbell, Clifford J., and Edward Marciniak. "A Report to the Mayor and City Council of Chicago on the Present Status and Effectiveness of Existing Fair Housing Practices Legislation in the United States as of April 1, 1963." Chicago Commission on Human Relations, 1963.

Coughlin, Frances. "A Conceptual Scheme for the Analysis of the Work of Intergroup Agencies." Unpublished paper, University of Washington, 1962.

Cressey, Paul F. "The Succession of Cultural Groups." Unpublished Ph.D. thesis, University of Chicago, 1930.

Donaldson, Charlotte, and George F. Ferguson. "Progress Report on an Exploratory Survey of the Differentiation of Function and Role of Human Relations Agencies and Their Interaction." Unpublished research project, University of Washington, 1961.

Fei, John Ching Han. "Rent Differentiation Related to Segregated Housing Markets for Racial Groups—With Special Reference to Seattle, Washington." Unpublished M.A. thesis, University of Washington, 1949.

Heim, Elizabeth E. "A Study of the Adjustment Problems of Negro Families Who Have Settled in White Neighborhoods in the Pittsburgh Area, and the Attitudes of Their White Neighbors." Unpublished tutorial study, Chatham College, Pittsburgh, Penn., April 20, 1959.

Henderson, Marjorie, Walter Hundley, and Thelma Jackson. *Three Research Studies on Race and Housing.* Unpublished M.A. thesis, University of Washington, 1963.

March, Sue. "AFSC Interviewing Project." Seattle, Wash. (mimeo), March 17-19, 1961.

———. "AFSC Interviewing Project." Seattle, Wash. (mimeo), Jan. 19-21, 1962.

Meadow, Kathryn P. "Negro-White Differences Among Newcomers to a Transitional Urban Area." Merrill-Palmer Institute (mimeo), 1962.

Noel, Donald Leroy. "Correlates of Anti-White Prejudice: Attitudes of Negroes in Four American Cities." Unpublished Ph.D. thesis, Cornell University, 1961.

Northwood, L. K. "Social Work in the Amelioration of Social Problems in the Inner City, a First Step toward Defining a Small Area Approach." Unpublished paper, University of Washington, 1962.

Palmer, Stuart H. "The Role of the Real Estate Agent in the Structuring of Residential Areas." Unpublished Ph.D. thesis, Yale University, 1955.

Schmid, Calvin F. Summary from "Impact of Recent Negro Migration on Seattle Schools." Paper presented at the International Population Conference in Vienna, 1959.

Selltiz, Claire, and Stuart W. Cook. "An Evaluation of the Probable Impact of Various Types of Action to Encourage Interracial Neighborhoods." Unpublished paper submitted to the Commission on Race and Housing, n.d.
———. "Factors Influencing Actions Regarding Interracial Neighborhoods." Unpublished paper submitted to the Commission on Race and Housing, March, 1957.
———. "How People Feel and Act about Interracial Housing." Unpublished paper submitted to the Commission on Race and Housing, 1957.
Wallace, David A. "Residential Concentration of Negroes in Chicago." Unpublished Ph.D. thesis, Harvard University, 1953.

OFFICIAL RECORDS

Hearings Before the United States Commission on Civil Rights— Housing. Hearings held in New York, Feb. 2-3, 1959, and Chicago, Ill., May 5-6, 1959. Washington, D.C.: Government Printing Office, 1959.
Mayor's Advisory Committee on Minority Housing. Hearings. Seattle, Wash. (tape recordings), Oct. 19, 1962.
O'Meara v. Washington State Board Against Discrimination, 58 Wn. 2d 793,365 P. 2d1 (1961).
United States Army Western Defense Command and Fourth Army. Japanese in the United States. Final Report. *Japanese Evacuation from the West Coast.* Washington, D.C.: Government Printing Office, 1943.
United States Bureau of the Census. *U.S. Census of Population: 1950, Census Tracts, Seattle, Washington.* Bulletin P-D 51. Washington, D.C.: Government Printing Office, 1952.
———. *U.S. Censuses of Population and Housing: 1960, Census Tracts, Seattle, Washington.* Final Report PHC (1)—142. Washington, D.C.: Government Printing Office, 1962.